Bode/Kühnel

ANTIQUE RUGS FROM THE NEAR EAST

ANTIQUE RUGS
FROM THE NEAR EAST

Wilhelm von Bode and Ernst Kühnel

Fourth, revised edition,
translated by
Charles Grant Ellis

LONDON: G. BELL & SONS 1970

First published in Great Britain 1970 by
G. Bell & Sons Ltd.,
6 Portugal Street,
London, W.C.2.

ISBN O 7135 16 16 X
Printed in Germany
Copyright by Klinkhardt & Biermann, Braunschweig

CONTENTS

FOREWORD TO THE FOURTH EDITION

When this handbook appeared in its original form, more than fifty years ago (1902), it was the first comprehensive treatise on the classic periods of the Oriental art of weaving knotted rugs. Since that time great folios with color plates of outstanding pieces, museum and exhibition catalogues as well as basic studies of various individual districts have been published from time to time, quite apart from the many books which essentially are concerned with more recent fashions in carpet manufacture. As an accurate and concise monographic treatment of the products of the golden age of the Near East, this volume still occupies to this day a lonely and distinctive niche amid a vast burgeoning of rug publications.

The second edition (1914), for which the undersigned became responsible, brought improvements and additions; the third (1922) further changes and an American version as translated by R. M. Riefstahl which was issued simultaneously with it. Both of these have been sold out long since and research developments have rendered them obsolete.

Consequently, an intensive recasting was required before the issuance of the fourth edition which we now submit, in order that this handbook might fulfill its proper mission, and the undersigned believes that this metamorphosis has been carried into effect in much the same way as the book's originator, who died in 1929, might have handled this problem. Those readers who are acquainted with the previous editions will note decided changes in the general arrangement, as well as in the treatment of individual chapters. They will also appreciate that Dr. Bode's vivid and scholarly presentation, especially in the introduction and in the final summing-up as well, has been preserved as carefully as seemed practicable with such timely changes and additions as might be needful.

We request the critical reader to indulge us once more in our fixed policy of the elimination of all footnotes, references to authorities and the like, just as we have done previously. On the other hand, a bibliography of the most important works on the subject has been included as essential.

A return to the earlier form of presentation reunites text with illustrations chapter by chapter whereas in the third edition the publisher had elected to segregate them in separate sections of the book.

As all of the old plates had been destroyed, the illustrative material had to be set up afresh and the result of this opportunity for reconsideration has been that no more than a good third of the subjects previously employed have been retained. All else is new with this volume, above all a greater accent upon the reproduction of carpets in paintings, a matter of singular importance in the classification of patterns as to the time of their occurrence. We have resisted the temptation to provide a greater number of color reproductions in order to keep publication costs within reasonable bounds; occasional references to colored plates in the big folios must suffice instead.

The carpets illustrated, with some exceptions, have been preserved intact. However for greater clarity the cuts will frequently show only so much of the original as may seem requisite for proper comprehension of the design. When fragmentary pieces are dealt with, this fact will be expressly pointed out. The current status of ownership of many rugs unfortunately cannot readily be determined, due to repeated changes.

Hispano-Moresque rugs have been excluded, for they form no proper portion of our subject, "Near Eastern Carpets"; those from Egypt, on the other hand, must remain in the picture because of their close relationships with the other groups and inasmuch as the origin attributed to them here has not yet been accepted by all authorities.

The undersigned is greatly indebted to Dr. Maurice S. Dimand (New York), M. Félix Guicherd (Lyons), Dr. Dora Heinz (Vienna) and Mr. Joseph V. McMullan (New York) for their suggestions of useful references and for much friendly assistance in the procurement of illustrative material.

Ernst Kühnel

Foreword to the English Edition

Mr. Ellis undertook the translation of the 4th edition upon his own initiative and has carried out this difficult task in such a perfect way that all those interested in an English version of this handbook will feel obliged to him for his devoted work.

The undersigned, moreover, must acknowledge with gratitude a number of valuable contributions by the translator concerning the ownership of certain pieces as well as other very useful statements. Together with critical remarks made by distinguished colleagues they have enabled the author to correct errors and to introduce improvements.

Thus, the present text can profess to be somewhat more up to date when compared with that of the German edition of 1955.

Berlin, February 1958

Ernst Kühnel

Preface by the Translator

This venture began with the simple intention of providing the writer and one or two of his friends with a more or less accurate working text for study and appreciation of an indispensable and basic handbook. There had been such obvious and radical changes in the composition of the fourth and present edition that the late Dr. Riefstahl's interpretation could no longer be considered adequate for the purpose.

When some distance along with the work, the translator felt encouraged to expand his original aim by planning to make his product available in some limited form to the inimitable and unfathomable brotherhood of the Hajji Baba Club. He is very glad indeed that a far wider circulation is now provided for "Vorderasiatische Knüpfteppiche" in its most modern guise.

The desire has been to present the Bode-Kühnel book not as a literal, word by word transcription but to make it a readable and enjoyable version of whatever rug-wisdom and information these two eminent authors have desired to impart to us.

The writer's deficiencies in dealing with an unfamiliar tongue have been largely compensated by Dr. Kühnel's kindness in revising his rough copy.

The author has taken this opportunity to make various alterations in his text and additions to his bibliography, as with the lapse of several years since the appearance of this edition in Germany new data have come to hand and there have been slight changes of viewpoint in certain respects.

In the highly debatable field of the spelling of Eastern proper names the translator has tried to choose the form which would be most likely to be familiar to most readers from their previous literary experience, although he is well aware that in several cases a different form will be considered more correct by purists.

He has also added a few notes of his own at the end of the book, hoping thereby to throw additional light upon certain matters.

Kingston, N. Y., February, 1958

Charles Grant Ellis

INTRODUCTION

The originator of this manual, Dr. Bode, could still recall very distinctly the impression which had been made upon him by the introduction into Germany of the carpets of "Old Persia" by agents of foreign firms during the seventies of the last century. Artists were the first to eject their dull and insipid Brussels carpets in favor of these lively, colorful products of the East, and the art-loving public was not slow in following their example. They all could feel very proud if they were able to acquire a few cheerful little prayer rugs and employ them as table-covers, as scatter rugs, or as throws for couches and as coverings for pillows. They thought themselves indeed fortunate to possess these valued specimens of the famous old "Persian knotted work" as such pieces were termed when they first made their appearance in the shops.

Such keen interest in Oriental rugs and an awakening pleasure in the use of color in household decoration shortly led the antiquarian trade to serious consideration of such genuinely antique examples as occasionally came to light in various places: in the Orient itself, especially in Turkey, and then, from time to time, in Italy, Spain and Portugal. Certain wealthy collectors proved to be the most avid early customers for costly rugs of silk, especially those who laid particular stress upon the magnificence of their homes. To decorate their studios artists snapped up the woolen carpets which came into the trade at quite trifling prices in Spain, South Germany and Italy (as a rule they had been withdrawn from use in church or palace there on account of their more or less mutilated condition), while others could be disposed of readily piece by piece to various museums.

In this way the investigation of Oriental rugs gradually developed greater precision and scholars began to enter into a serious study of these weavings, although at first in but a hit-or-miss and hesitant manner. Students soon became convinced that those pieces which were brought to market directly from the East in such great numbers were, with few exceptions, strictly of modern origin. On the other hand, old paintings frequently were found to include the likenesses of carpets which were related closely indeed both in design and color to various actual rugs then to be seen in the antique trade. Philological research applied itself to scrutiny of the inscriptions which appear on many rugs, sought to determine their true age from such likely evidence, and set out to extract from these texts whatever they might contain in the way of genuine ancient information.

Convincing data also were obtained through comparisons of the decorative schemes of these textiles with design motives which were to be found in architecture, miniature paintings, metalwork, pottery and other manifestations of Oriental industry. Moreover, in order to pin-point the origins of old examples, close attention was paid to the modern rugs which were being imported from the various regions of the Near and Middle East, especially by the great carpet firms which caused them to be bought up in the bazaars or else woven there on speculation. Most of all, interest and understanding in this sphere were advanced by more frequent displays of rugs, notably the great Vienna Carpet Exhibition of 1891 and its attendant publication, a masterpiece truly founded upon bedrock, which was followed in 1907 by a supplementary volume. In 1908 came Martin's splendid carpet history and in 1912 the folio of the Munich Islamic Exhibition of 1910. Then in 1926—28 there appeared a true chef d'oeuvre of reproduction technique, the "Altorientalische Teppiche" by Sarre and Trenkwald, and finally in 1938 Arthur Upham Pope has provided us with a still more extensive and essential enrichment of our knowledge in his "Survey of Persian Art".

Among the several methods of inquiry, one might well suppose that the most rewarding and most accurate would be through the study of inscriptions, as is the case with Islamic buildings, metalwork and the like. Yet this very method up to this point has proved to be distinctly unsuccessful when it has not been utterly unreliable. Up to the present time scarce a dozen classic carpets have been found to bear dates which we may consider authentic. The efforts which have been made with the outlay of much scholarship to authenticate more fully certain other weavings which appear either with dates or with inscribed texts which seem to offer support for their chronology constantly have been proved open to grave doubt, or indeed actually misleading in some cases; on such grounds 19th century copies and trifling late pieces have solemnly been pronounced to be works of half a thousand years of age. The basis for this particular phenomenon lies in the exceptional difficulties which we encounter as soon as we start to investigate in this field. It is not merely that inscriptions of this sort are most unusual and when present often difficult to read; their sense too is never easy to interpret unless (as is customary) they consist of unimportant passages from the Koran, adages or secular verses. We must bear in mind also that many rugs, especially those intended for religious purposes, have been copied, together with their inscriptions, repeatedly over the course of the centuries, with particular care in recent times, thus creating an additional complication.

Far more accurate assistance towards our determination of the age and the locale of ancient carpets than has been furnished us up to now by this linguistic dissection of inscriptions is provided by stylistic studies of the parallels between these age-old knotted fabrics and the products of the various other Near Eastern crafts in view of the precise dating which is found so frequently among the latter and because of the simultaneous appearance of the same decorative forms in certain periods in certain areas both in the rugs and in other artifacts. Here too our research encounters certain limitations which, far too easily overlooked, may entail a chain of erroneous conclusions. When specific details which result from the technique employed have once come into use; from that time on they will recur on the most diverse occasions, frequently with modifications which are scarcely noticeable. In this respect the art of the Orient exhibits a highly exceptional sense of conservatism: for instance, decorative themes which we find in the very oldest weavings of the Eastern countries have been preserved with more or less fidelity through thousands of years right up to the present day despite the fearful and well-nigh elemental upheavals of tribal existence, which these particular sections of the world have experienced time and again, and quite regardless of the turbulent conditions that have been their inevitable aftermath. These catastrophic tribal tumults and wars, which had extreme effects upon both art and the crafts and involved them in a regular and continuous series of upward and downward surges, repeatedly evoked similar phenomena in the weaving of textiles as well. First would come a thorough demoralization, followed by a gradual awakening which, availing itself of the bases of old traditions and models, asserts itself at various times in a like manner in the design and execution of rugs as well. This renders recognition more difficult, especially for earlier periods, whether this pattern or that one in some specific carpet exhibits the tainted and barbarous forms of decadence or the primitive and powerful elements of an artistic vigor which is just in the process of reawakening. In this way the careless and misconstrued imitations of a later age are frequently taken for the creations of primitive art practices and, conversely, characteristic works of earlier epochs upon occasion have been estimated as degenerate.

In attempts to unravel the history of rug knotting much attention has also been paid to the study of modern carpet weaving in the Near East. It long was hoped that from the designs which are in current use among the weavers of the various districts of Asia Minor, Kurdistan, Persia, Turkestan, Caucasia and other areas traditions regarding the continuity of old patterns might gradually be confirmed, and that through the application of such data the very regions and districts in which these old designs were actually fabricated might be ferreted out. Whatever has been accomplished to date in this field, however, has by no means come up to expectations. To be sure we will constantly hear suggestions from the dealer who perceives at once in any old rug a related modern design with which he happens to be conversant. Accordingly, quite innocent of historic backgrounds, he will cheerfully identify the spot where the new piece was manufactured as the birthplace of the analogous old pattern as well. Inferences along this line, however, must be drawn with the greatest of caution and then only if a century-long tradition can be established for the weaving of knotted carpets in the city or district in question. Many Near Eastern peoples have always led a nomadic life. At various times they have undergone prodigious dislodgements and migrations and have been subjected to dreadful disasters which frequently have wiped out entire tribes and their homes together. On the other hand the ancient and little-altered trade routes with their heavy traffic have existed there for thousands of years back into time. It seems quite plausible that these several factors would have resulted in the cessation of an old weaving in one locality as a matter of course and the simultaneous transference and resurrection of this well-known design in other regions which often were quite widely separated both from each other and from the first. We shall see later on that this actually can be demonstrated for a whole series of the most interesting rug types. In this field therefore a comparative study of region and place still invites approach from well-nigh every standpoint.

One might well suppose that the reproduction of carpets in those Persian miniature paintings which have become so widely known in the

14

course of the past few decades would offer momentous disclosures toward their classification historically. Sad to say, however, the rewards of investigation in this quarter have proved to be astonishingly meager. The primary reason for this has been that as the Persian painters seldom worried themselves about the absolute accuracy of their rug designs, far more often than not these have suffered changes in ornamental significance when they have not simply been invented offhand. Conversely, the examination of such examples as occur in European paintings has proved to be one of the most dependable and fruitful sources of knowledge of the carpets of the Near East and of their development. The hints they offer regarding the evolution of the ancient carpet industry in the Near East will form the most satisfactory foundation for the essay in hand aside from exploration of the surviving originals themselves. Furthermore this study will prove to be of singular interest to us in that from it we can learn something of the importance which these carpets together with other Oriental textiles have held for the West; not merely because of their effect upon its handicrafts, but through their impact even upon its fine arts. This came about as a consequence of their influence upon the development of the great coloristic schools of painting, particularly the Venetian and to some degree the Dutch School as well.

It is well known historically how accessible Venice became to Oriental art through its close communications with the Levant. A glance at Venetian paintings of the 15th century will show us that City of Lagoons even in those days still in semi-Oriental garb. In representations of Venetian festivals and processions, in those numerous paintings which offer us views of the city or else subjects from the interiors of its houses, rugs from the East hang down as holiday decorations from window and balcony; carpets serve as floor-coverings in private homes as well as in the public palaces and lie as spreads upon the tables; even the very gondolas were covered over and decked out with rugs. The churches too in particular were richly blessed with them: upon the steps of the altars, before the seats of the ecclesiastics and over the balustrades lay the glorious carpets of the Levant, providing an exquisite feast for the eyes of the most penniless Venetian. Just as in those days a flourishing and artistic handicraft was developed in Venice itself in order to supply the luxurious fabrics, the glasswares, vessels of inlaid metal, worked leathers and all the other items of household furniture which for centuries had been imported from the East or else had been manufactured by Mohammedan artisans in the Turkish Quarter of Venice (later in the Fondaco de' Turchi), so also was this environment mirrored simultaneously in the eye of the painter. From a style of painting characterized by sober and neutral tints there was developed in the course of a few decades the most magnificent school for coloring that art has yet produced. Anyone who is familiar with the Oriental rugs of the 15th century will sense in the selection of hues and their juxtaposition in the paintings of contemporary Venetians a similar color perception to that of the carpets. Only under the masters of the 16th century, primarily Giorgione and Titian, was painting released from this dependence upon the artistic crafts of the East and rendered fully self-sufficient.

Just as in this instance Venetian art through its drafts upon the Orient and upon the color harmonies of Near Eastern rugs in particular, even when these pieces themselves have not been introduced into the paintings, still seems to be essentially in accord with them in coloristic bent, two centuries later the East demonstrates afresh its peculiar animating powers in the evolution of color trends on this side of the Alps. This is the case with the Flemish and to a still higher degree with the Dutch School. Although in the course of the 16th century through Spanish influence numerous products of the Orient, carpets especially, had been imported here in quite a roundabout manner, in the following century direct trade with Persia as well as with the commercial settlements in the Near East brought a veritable host of rugs to the Netherlands. In what numbers Persian rugs were to find employment as table-covers or as floor-pieces in the homes of the burghers is apparent from a glance at the manifold reproductions of Dutch interiors. And above all were they acceptable to artists as customary household decoration, as one may venture to conclude from the frequent occurrence in their paintings of these Oriental patterns in all their diversity. Just as the eye of the Dutch painter was influenced involuntarily by having these colorful objects constantly about him, in England too from this time on this new desire to adorn one's own home with Oriental rugs (whose production was now stimulated to yet another climax by the Englishmen themselves) maintained more firmly a feeling for color, for strong yet harmonious tints, than in Germany where during the first half of the last century this scheme gives way to a flagrant garishness, and then later on to a tiresome sort of tonal stupor, defects over which our most recent art movement alone has sought to prevail. To this a more intensive preoccupation with the art of the Orient has again made notable contributions.

The assumption that no more than a scattering of pieces of truly early Oriental knotted weaving have been preserved until our day, which was advanced by J. Lessing in his well-known rug publication ("Ancient Oriental Carpet Designs", 1877), the very first to stimulate the scholarly treatment of this question, and to which Riegl too adhered in his handbook on old Oriental rugs (1891), has been refuted even for the public at large by the celebrated and marvelous exhibition of carpets at the Commercial Museum in Vienna in 1891, by the display of masterpieces of Islamic art at Munich in 1910 and through more recent arrangements by which hundreds of "antique" carpets have been shown. The abundance of these examples and their high degree of diversity have however by no means led to agreement even among experts regarding the weighty questions of their antiquity and their origins; among many it seemed rather to induce a fatalistic resignation to the impossibility of finding any solution which would be conclusive. Really the situation is by no means so unfavorable. After all we do have sufficient trustworthy evidence to enable us to date carpets and if we cannot do so within the year or even the decade in most cases, at least we can establish the proper century in every instance. In order to attain lucidity in this regard, certainly first of all one must disencumber his mind of the innumerable mass of petty and superficially picturesque weavings of the end of the 18th and of the 19th centuries, charming as some of these may be, as well as recent imitations and counterfeits. He must rather seek to acquire an intimacy with such truly antique material as may still be extant and available for study in museums, palaces, church treasuries, in private ownership and in the art trade.

One of the most extensive collections of old Oriental carpets and one of the most interesting too for the number of early works which it included, was that of the Islamic section of the Berlin Museum and this regrettably has suffered important losses through bombing raids in the course of the Second World War. Of greater importance and noteworthy for their clever presentation are the treasures of the Austrian Museum for Art and Industry in Vienna; still more numerous those of the Victoria & Albert Museum in London and the holdings, for the most part unpublished, of the Museum of Turkish and Islamic Art in Istanbul. Among public European collections, notably splendid and important pieces are owned also by the National

Museum at Munich, the Louvre, the Museum of Decorative Arts and that of the Gobelins in Paris, the Textile Museum at Lyons, the Poldi-Pezzoli Museum in Milan, the Bardini Museum at Florence and the Hermitage at Leningrad. Characteristic examples are offered also to those whose interest as students is more acute by the Rijksmuseum in Amsterdam, the Museum of Ancient Art in Lisbon and the museum at Coimbra in Portugal, as well as by various museums of the industrial arts (Berlin, Leipzig, Düsseldorf, Budapest, Copenhagen etc.). In Italian churches (Padua Cathedral, St. Mark's at Venice, S. Francesco at Brescia) and in Spanish monasteries one still can find an occasional carpet of the classic period, but normally in religious places this heritage, originally esteemed, was squandered little by little as the years went by.

In our own century American museums have taken the lead in the acquisition of antique Oriental carpets and the advantage which they have won in this respect becomes yearly more apparent. At the peak stand the Metropolitan Museum in New York with several dozen carpets of the very highest order and the Textile Museum in Washington, founded by G. H. Myers, whose holdings quantitatively are even more extensive. In third place we must mention Philadelphia, to which McIlhenny and Williams entrusted their collections, but St. Louis, Cincinnati, Detroit, Cleveland, Boston and Los Angeles have also secured for themselves many interesting examples. In the Orient itself the Islamic Museum in Cairo deserves mention before all others.

A thorough redistribution has taken effect among such items as were formerly in private hands. Most of the rug treasures which had for centuries past been the property of German, Austrian and English noble families have now changed ownership, and private collections once of significant repute (Goupil, Yerkes, Ballard, Figdor, Sarre, Cassirer, Widener, Clark etc.) long since have passed out of existence. In the U.S.A. they are largely a thing of the past, their contents having come under museum control. The brilliant collection brought together by J. V. McMullan even now is undergoing this process. It is doubtful if any systematic collectors of rugs in the grand style are still to be found in Europe, and likewise in America we know of no new names which we can add at the present time. In the same way the ranks of the great dealers have almost completely vanished away; Bernheimer in Munich to be sure still has a very valuable stock of old pieces and in New York Karekin Beshir has stepped into the limelight in recent years.

Closer study of such collective material as has been preserved yields a very limited number of carpet types which have been repeated with slight variations and whose genesis or development through the course of two or three centuries can be authenticated by means of their portrayal in old paintings. Certain of these classes were disseminated so widely and maintained themselves over so long a period that many dozens of specimens of these types are still to be found whereas others occur but rarely and perhaps were woven only to fill unusual requirements. To be sure the supply of originals at hand is quite insufficient for a complete history of the art of knotting in the Near East, and for this we perhaps will always lack the necessary foundations. For all that, most of the surviving antique specimens date from the 16th to the 18th centuries, and some go right back into the fifteenth; up to now but a handful of pieces are known which could be assigned to a period still earlier. We can follow them as far back as the close of the 13th century through paintings and miniatures. On the other hand the sporadic carpet-like representations to be seen on Sassanid silver bowls or Assyrian reliefs are not to be claimed forthwith as knotted fabrics, for they probably were executed in kilim technique, embroidery or appliqué, and the presumption which was originally urged upon us as result of a sensational discovery in the Altai region not long ago, that carpets were knotted as early as the 5th century B.C., requires more thorough future examination. The accounts of the writers of yesteryear regarding the carpets of the early Middle Ages either are too ill-defined or else are tricked out too richly with the flowery language of the Orient for us to be able to evoke a reasonably trustworthy conception of the originals. And now with this we have well-nigh exhausted the sources from which we might more closely acquaint ourselves with the early history of Near Eastern knotted carpets; these sources provide us with but the barest of frameworks for our study of the continuity of their development. In consequence, our opinion must be that we can scarcely expect proofs of a historically arranged sequence prior to more recent times when among the shadows of earlier ages only a few weak and vague flickerings of light in this regard have been preserved.

We have excluded from our survey all manner of tapestries, pillow-covers and the like, for in the Orient in former times just as today the knotted rug, if we disregard the hanging carpets which at times are to be observed in the mosques, served exclusively as a floor covering. Costly carpets lay then and still do this very day in the center of the room, so that one's glance, roving over the seat-cushions which run along the walls, will come to rest upon this precious item, the pride of the house. As a rule the room's traffic passes over narrow but stouter woolen runners which lie on both sides of the central and most important piece.

As to the technique of the knotting we have referred in previous editions to A. Riegl's book on knotted carpets, pioneer in its day, but now antiquated and moreover incomplete in its description of the process. For the reader of this English edition we think it more appropriate to quote some passages from A. U. Dilley's outline:

> "To tie a knot a weaver, quicker than it can be told, passes an end of dyed yarn between two adjacent warp strings, around one and over and under the other, snaps the two loops into the line of weaving, and severs the projecting yarn with the stroke of a knife; or passes the yarn end between two warp, around one and merely under the other. ... Maximum speed is approximately fifteen knots a minute, which sustained is nine hundred knots an hour.
>
> Knots are tied in rows, one to each pair of strings, and bound in horizontal ranks by a cross yarn, called weft, which is run through the warp strings above each row of knots. Compactness is attained by hammering down the rows as each is completed. Infrequently, four to six rows of knots will be tied before a weft is inserted, and again as many as six wefts will be used to each row of knots. The former procedure sacrifices strength to fineness, the latter fineness to strength.
>
> The knots are of two kinds, single and double, the former called Persian or Sehna, and the latter Turkish or Ghiordes. Unfortunately these names are misleading and inadequate. They are misleading because they create the impression that Persian rugs are woven in the Persian knot, which is true and false. ... The names are inadequate because they leave out of account the character of the knotting practised in the other rug-weaving countries. ... Speculation as to the ancient source of these knots, and as to how the cleavage of Asia by them came about, is instantly enveloped in utter darkness. ..."
> (pp. 251, 252).

Mr. Dilley proposes that we distinguish rather between "Near East Knot", practised west of the Caspian Sea, and "Far East Knot" used east of the

Caspian. This too is unsuitable, for the "Far East Knot" is the custom of weavers in many districts of Western Iran, and notably at Senna itself, the famous carpet center in Kurdistan. (By the way, the only correct spelling is "Senna", "Sinneh" or "Senne"; "Sehna" or "Sahna" — pronounced with an emphatic "h" — being the name of another place in Persia, which has no rug industry at all). W. Grote-Hasenbalg recommends "full knot" for the Ghiordes and "half knot" for the Senna variety, terms which would be technically justified.

As a matter of fact, among the ancient rugs which we are studying here all Anatolian and Caucasian groups are woven in the so-called Ghiordes knot, all Egyptian and nearly all Persian products, moreover those from Turkestan and India, in the so-called Senna manner. A third species, the so-called Spanish knot, tied to only one warp, we do not take into consideration as it has no bearing upon the topic in hand. For further technical details we refer the reader to C. E. C. Tattersall's excellent "Notes on carpet-knotting and weaving", published by the Victoria & Albert Museum in 1933.

In conclusion something still remains to be said in our general survey regarding the significance of field and border. Field design in carpets evolved from the original idea of a textile pattern which might be prolonged endlessly without variation, and in most classes it has followed this decorative principle regardless of the differences in form which these repeat motives might assume. Only in Persia and in India were pictorially balanced compositions adopted for which the borders might fulfill the same office as a frame does for a painting, whereas usually the surface pattern was simply cut off by a border which was itself hemmed in by narrow guard stripes. In their drawing these borders maintain complete independence from the fields, as a rule have been kept in contrast to these in color too, and especially in the carpets of the classical period greater value was placed upon an effective separation of the two elements of the design. The Persians paid great regard moreover to elegant solutions for their corners, while the Anatolian Turks concerned themselves not at all with this problem, but simply permitted the horizontal and vertical framing stripes to butt one against the other.

THE CARPETS OF TURKEY

Early Anatolian Rugs

Among the nomadic tribes of Turkestan the weaving of knotted carpets was a familiar skill from the very beginning, and their geometrically patterned weavings still reveal today, aside from expert execution, the tradition of extremely old and simple decorative principles. Hence it is not particularly surprising that in this region, in Eastern Turkestan in fact, the first evidences of the early advent of the technique of knotting should have

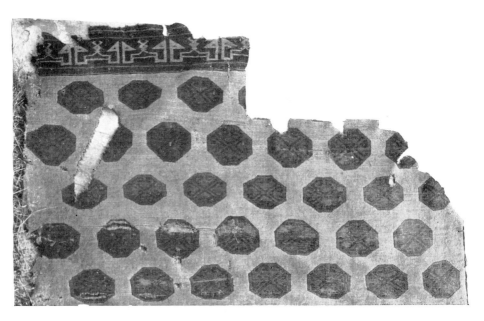

1. Rug from Konia   *Museum of Islamic Art, Istanbul*

been discovered. These are among the findings of the Turfan Expedition of the Berlin Museum and the fruits of the explorations of Marc Aurel Stein and could well have originated in the 5th or 6th century A. D. at the very

22

latest. Perhaps they go back somewhat farther still. Unfortunately, the fragments provide us with no clear information regarding their designs.

How and when the technique then succeeded in spreading all the way accross to the Near East completely evades our knowledge as yet. Neither

2. Rug from Konia   *Museum of Islamic Art, Istanbul*

dependable literary sources nor surviving examples remain at our disposal from the centuries that ensued. Probably in the beginning the products of the Turkoman nomads came into trade only in scant volume; for ordinary requirements reed mats and kilims had to suffice as floor covering. The vogue for carpets in the grand manner must have been first adopted by the Seljuks who in the 11th century were hurled out of their ancestral homes in Turkestan only to attain sovereignty over the entire Near East, and as sequel to these events came the establishment of whole families of rug-weavers in the cities of Persia and Asia Minor. Be that as it may, that branch of the Turkish peoples which became resident in Anatolia were in the first rank of contributors to the true development of style in carpets. Actually this had already attained full bloom by the time of the Sultanate of Konia; for Marco Polo, who visited the realm of the Seljuks at the end of the 13th century, makes mention of the fact that here the finest and most beautiful carpets were produced.

By great good fortune we possess several specimens which may be reconciled with such reports. These lay in the pillared hall of the Mosque of Alâ ed-dîn in Konia, for which they evidently were made, until they were removed to the Museum of Turkish and Islamic Art in Istanbul. Five of them are certainly homogeneous and must have been woven at the very end of the 13th century. They have been carefully executed in the typical Turkish knotting and, too, they are so effectively blended in their coloring that they are by no means to be regarded as primitive productions; the same applies to the varied draftsmanship in every respect. One of these pieces (Fig. 1) displays staggered rows of octagons containing floral ornament; the others have for field decoration a uniformly continuous interlace or trellis pattern set out so as to form stars or lozenges. The border is composed either of extremely stylized and eccentric, at times quite heavy Cufic script (Fig. 3) or of star-rosettes in a linear setting (Fig. 2). To the Konia series must be added several additional fragments, first disclosed in 1929 and obviously contemporary, from the Mosque of Beyshehir, located in the same district. The largest of these presents a patterning of continuous, strongly stylized arabesques with, on the other hand, a very individual two-part border. We have a ready verification for the precise dating of the Konia group in one of Giotto's frescoes. This he carried out at Padua in the Arena Chapel about 1304 and in it a carpet fully analogous to the one which we reproduce in Fig. 2 serves as an altar decoration. Probably the master used as his model one of the rugs which, according to a surviving document which deals with the consecration of the edifice in 1305, were placed at the disposal of the local authorities by Venice. Evidently by this time these pieces must already be considered as export merchandise. As to whether the related patterns of the hangings in several of Giotto's earlier paintings in the Lower Church at Assisi likewise

3. Rug from Konia
Museum of Islamic Art, Istanbul

24

sprang from such a stimulus, we still cannot venture an opinion. Close relationships exist also with carpets which are shown in Persian illuminations of the 14th and 15th centuries (see below, p. 85), and this type has its continuation in the Hispano-Moresque weavings of the 14th to the 15th century, as whose proto-types they doubtless must be considered, but this forms no part of our current theme.

It is quite possible that in the 14th century animal forms also may have found their place in the weaver's range of representational conception. Naturally these forms were expressed at first, however, still in a most strictly linear style. We possess clear testimony for this in a fragmentary rug which, discovered in a church in Middle Italy, was acquired in Rome and now belongs to the Islamic Department in Berlin (Fig. 4). Both of the panels which it still displays (inasmuch as the border is present along only one of the long sides, it is possible that it originally comprised four, or more probably six panels) have the same design: the dragon in combat with the phoenix, in a

4. Animal Rug (fragment) *State Museums, Berlin*

linear draftsmanship which may appear barbaric, yet is extremely suitable stylistically; the framing of the octagonal panels and the narrow borders are of simple, rigid geometric forms. The colors are just as modest as they are forceful: the ground is a hearty yellow, the animals are red with blue details, the border has red ornamentation upon a *tête de nègre* ground.

25

In a publication on old Norwegian carpet designs we find a similar piece; certain peculiarities indicate that this is not of Oriental workmanship, but it is so closely related to the Near Eastern knotted fabric just described and in both its arrangement and its decor it strikes such a vivid note of the Oriental right on down to individual details that in our opinion it can only be regarded as a copy of a similar knotted rug.

A fortunate chain of events has preserved for us in old illustrations this very carpet, which until not long ago stood quite by itself as an isolated phenomenon; and these render us support in our determination of its time of origin. The most important of these is to be found in the Spedale della Scala in Siena in the fresco "The Wedding of the Foundlings" by Domenico

5. Detail from a Painting at Siena by Domenico di Bartolo   *Anderson Photo*

di Bartolo, which can be dated between 1440 and 1444 (Fig. 5). The panel design is almost identical, is stylized in the same manner, and is repeated at least six times with the corner ornamentation misunderstood and the borders perhaps arbitrarily interpreted and extended by the artist. The same rug with a different border treatment occurs in a Madonna by Baldovinetti (Jarves Collection, New Haven) and, repeated this time with only two panels, in a painting ascribed to D. Morone in the Este Collection at Vienna. A good many examples of this weaving must have been scattered about in Italy in the 15th century, it would seem. A second knotted rug which is closely related to the Berlin piece in technique and style first came to light three decades ago. It was found in the church at Marby (Sweden) and is now to be seen in the Historical Museum at Stockholm. It displays in each of its two octagonal panels, in stark geometric drawing, two birds which stand facing a bush; the spandrels have the same latch-hook ornamentation as in the other specimen, and the border and guards repeat an S-shaped

26

motive in various ways. We shall be obliged to date the Marby rug also as early as the 15th century.

However, in this matter of Anatolian animal rugs we are not limited to the two known survivals; additional designs, which have been compiled in a separate essay by K. Erdmann, are to be found also in a whole succession

6. Detail from a Madonna by Lippo Memmi   *Gemäldegalerie, Berlin*

of Italian paintings of the 15th and 14th centuries. The animals, whether quadrupeds or birds, appear singly or else in pairs, almost invariably in octagonal panels, and the entire composition follows the two originals which we have described so closely that we must consider these painted

rugs for the most part as prototypes of such actual relics, inasmuch as some of them go back to the beginning of the 14th century. The colors are bold and often are counterchanged from panel to panel; in the intersections of the framing-stripes we find little lozenges or swastikas. In one of these pictures, the "Betrothal of Mary" by the Sienese Niccolo di Buonaccorso at the National Gallery in London (No. 1109, painted about 1380), stand extremely stiff birds (eagles, it would seem) yellow or red in color, confronted upon a ground of red or yellow. A similar rug appears in a Madonna ascribed to Lippo Memmi in the Berlin

7. Detail from an Annunciation
Gemäldegalerie, Vienna

8. Detail from a Madonna by
A. Lorenzetti   *Helbing Auction, 1933*

27

Gallery (No. 1072, Fig. 6), which was executed in or about 1350. The panels here present in heraldic manner pairs of long-legged eagles together with a formalized tree; the framing and borders carry swastikas and skimpy ornaments. Decades earlier still (1317) is the large painting with St. Louis by Simone Martini in S. Lorenzo at Naples, with a rug upon whose every panel pairs of eagles are repeated. The same decoration appears also in a carpet in the triptych of the school of Giotto which is in the Sacristy of St. Peter's at Rome, and this likewise harks back to the early 14th century. Furthermore a rug with single birds in octagons is portrayed in the still somewhat older Annunciation painting in the Church of SSma Annunziata at Florence; but since this, as a religious treasure, is to be seen only during the annual celebrations and then but from a great distance, and inasmuch as the numerous copies (see among others Fig. 7) are themselves merely super-ficial, an accurate description is impossible. Among others we find stalking beasts of prey in alternated coloring as a carpet design (Fig. 8) in a Madonna ascribed to Ambrogio Lorenzetti.

When we attempt to translate into actual rug scale the extremely reduced versions which we have discovered in these early panels, we can preserve but an empty and jejune impression of their true designs. This is to be expected also when we deal with the precedents for the Konia designs, and so we must by no means assume that these close copies will reflect the originals exactly; for, as in their reproduction of other details, the men of the 14th century could scarcely have wished to give more than an indifferently accurate impression of the rugs as well. Therefore they felt quite free to neglect all minor accessories such as the patterns of borders and guards, the incidental ornamentation of the fields and the probable detailed drawing of the bodies of the animals, or else to barely indicate these in a superficial manner. Every building, each item of contemporary furniture, or textile pattern, or product of the minor arts that occurs in the paintings of Giotto and his successors represents merely an abridgement of the original, and therefore we must surely make the same assumption regarding the rugs as well whenever they appear at such an early date. On the other hand, when we deal with painters of the Quattrocento, who often took extreme pains to perfect the tiniest details, and who would scrupulously reproduce each brocade pattern in the raiment of the blessed, we can credit their rug representations also without question.

As concerns the precise origin of these carpets so immortalized by European painters, we must, generally speaking, restrict ourselves to the theory that these pieces naturally would have entered into the Italian commerce of the period from the more accessible provinces of the Near East, which would mean Asia Minor and Armenia, and in fact most probably from districts which did not lie far distant from the seacoasts. Writers of the 13th and of the 14th centuries who, alas, make but exceptional and fleeting mention of carpets, nevertheless name Anatolia explicitly as the home of a thriving carpet industry and speak of the exportation of its products from Asia Minor to Italy. Whether we are to accept this early category of rugs, including a few fragments which have been excavated in Fostât, as purely Anatolian weavings, or rather as the prototypes of the so-called Armenian animal carpets, of which we shall have something to say later on, and whether Transcaucasia is to be considered as the birth-place of this group — in contrast to the Konia series — still remains open to question.

The So-called Holbein Rugs

We have already learned that it was highly characteristic of the early animal carpets to interpret all motives in an austere, quite a mathematical manner, so to speak. There has existed in other instances a similar propensity for the transformation of the most diverse botanical forms into geometric patterning; often in these designs the blossoms and leaves cannot be clearly recognized just as was the case with the animals in the group mentioned above. The farther that we go back into the 16th century, the more forcefully does this tendency become evident, and in the 15th century it must have been quite universal. But to be sure even here the connection with plant life can always be established if only we look closely enough.

This applies with especial force to one design, and while this was in style innumerable examples of it were introduced into Europe, so that even now we can still cite hundreds of original specimens; it also appears far more frequently in old paintings than any other class of carpets. We can deduce from these illustrations a manufacture of exceptionally long duration in the course of which there was little modification of pattern; we can follow the series through two full centuries in this same fashion. In this

29

design there is spread a frozen net of creepers in shapes that are completely angular, with the mature flowers expressed as palmettes or rosettes and the arabesque as a constant factor. Its basic structure is quite similar to one that we have already mentioned at the beginning of our description of the animal rugs, and we shall find it repeated in still other groups: octagons in

9. So-called Holbein Rug (now missing)   *Formerly State Museums, Berlin*

square, or rather rectangular settings. The pattern covers the entire field like a lattice made of withes. In the earliest phase the border habitually presents ornamental pseudo-Cufic characters, which by degrees become a pure decoration of angular ribbonwork; later this is superseded by a frame composed of counterchanged panels with hard floral devices or a sparse leafy vine. Occasional use is also made of the cloud band instead. In the course of the 17th century the draftsmanship of the field, and that of the border as well, grows continually more crude and obscure, the knotting more loose and unsatisfactory.

Among this group we can distinguish three classes which all trace back to the same decorative principle, and this they interpret in varied terms

10. Detail from the Gisze Portrait by H. Holbein   *Gemäldegalerie, Berlin*

both as to composition and as to color. Two of these have — somewhat misleadingly — been designated as "Holbein carpets", due to the fact that

11. The "Somerset House Conference" (detail)
National Portrait Gallery, London

this master (as well as other painters, some of whom in fact were earlier) was exceptionally prone to introduce these types into his pictures. One of them is designed on a large scale and presents more variations. The patterning of the other is minutely drawn and it is more homogeneous. This second design displays in regular rows knotted motives derived from octagons, each with an inner star, set in diamonds, and stylized tendrils at the points of intersection as well as little stars filling in between. The border normally has a delicate ribbon-interlace in white against a colored ground. Originally this was in the form of intelligible pseudo-Cufic letters, later it was composed as pure filleting; from time to time little polygons with knots or rosettes appear, employed in alternation

31

with stars, or again in earlier versions sometimes a wiry foliate scroll. The guard stripes now and then display a reciprocal ornament reminiscent of certain wall-crestings.

This class of rugs (Fig. 9, Pl. I), of striking coloring (usually on a dark red ground) and careful knotting, undoubtedly offers bases for comparison with certain West Turkestan weavings which have probably experienced a similar evolution. This type may be followed in paintings from about the middle of the 15th until deep into the 16th century; predominantly in the Italian, but in some German works as well. A few of the most significant, in which the design of the rugs is particularly easy to recognize, are enumerated herewith: Mantegna's celebrated Madonna in San Zeno at Verona of the year 1459, Carpaccio's Ursula Cycle (1495) in the Academy at Venice, Pinturicchio's frescoes of 1505 in the Library at Siena, a pair of paintings of the Madonna by Domenico Ghirlandaio in the Academy and the Uffizi at Florence (about 1480) and one by Seb. Mainardi in the Gallery at Naples, Raffaelino's early painting of the Madonna in the Berlin Gallery, the family portrait by Licinio Pordenone at Hampton Court (of the year 1524), Bassano's Madonna in the Pinakothek at Munich, H. Holbein's Georg Gisze portrait of 1532 in the Berlin Gallery (Fig. 10), Piero della Francesca's fresco in San Francesco at Rimini (of the year 1451), the Annunciation by Baldovinetti in San Miniato near Florence (about 1460), the early masterpiece by Credi in the Cathedral at Pistoia (about 1480), Ercole Roberti's Enthroned Madonna in the Brera at Milan (about 1480),

12. So-called Holbein Rug
Formerly Pohlmann Collection, Berlin

So-called Holbein Carpet (Detail)   *State Museums, Berlin*

certain paintings by Francesco Bonsignori and by Gaudenzio Ferrari, Mantegna's frescoes in the Castle at Mantua (soon after 1460), Badile's Madonna in the Museum at Verona (of 1546), a male portrait by

Parmegianino in the Museum at Naples, another by Dosso Dossi in the Corsini Gallery at Rome and that of a cardinal by Pontormo in the Borghese Gallery. A rug of this type, an echo of the older pattern, was reproduced with great accuracy yet again in the large group portrait of the Somerset House Conference, London 1604, in the National Portrait Gallery there, the work of M. Geeraerts, a Netherlander who was painting in England at the time (Fig. 11). So late an appearance for this type is readily explained, as the artist portrayed the honorable commissioners in a room in which the carpet might well have already served as a table-cover for a great many years.

13. So-called Holbein Rug (fragment)
Museum of Islamic Art, Istanbul

This class underwent little change in the course of a full century, except for minor variations. In former years original pieces often came to light in Italy and South Germany, but probably never appeared at all, on the other hand, in Spain, which by that time had already produced an important carpet industry of its own. Examples are to

be found in many European and American collections, and from time to time in the art trade as well. An interesting bit of evidence of the wide dissemination of these "Holbein rugs" is offered by pieces of European wool embroidery designed as wall-hangings,

14. Detail from a Painting by V. Foppa
The Brera, Milan

15. Detail from a Painting by D. Ghirlandaio
The Uffizi, Florence

more or less faithfully copied from such prototypes: two of these are in the Swiss National Museum at Zurich, dated 1533 and 1609; others are in the Museums of Decorative Arts in Nuremberg (dated 1605) and Leipzig (dated 1539) and in the Victoria and Albert Museum (dated 1603) as well.

We must consider as a variety of the group just described a series of rugs in which a like sense of draftsmanship tends to borrow from the same range of forms, with the distinction, however, that in this series the design is kept to a larger scale. In this case the entire field is taken up by just a few star forms in their

16. So-called Holbein Carpet   *State Museums, Berlin*

34

17. Turkish Arabesque Rug (Lotto Rug)
Formerly W. v. Bode, Berlin

octagonal settings, whereas in the other type these forms appeared in a more compact arrangement and were distinctly smaller in size, not standing out very prominently from the ground. Original pieces of this second sort are none too common (Figs. 12, 13); their more sprightly coloring is a departure from the others, which have a softer toning, and they have established a family tree among certain varieties of the so-called Bergama clan. These rugs too must be classed among the "Holbein carpets", for the master brought them also into his paintings (in addition to the rugs of smaller pattern which we mentioned a moment ago); they occur elsewhere chiefly

18. Detail from a Madonna by L. Longhi
Gemäldegalerie, Berlin

among the Flemings and Italians, and of course the conception is always highly geometric. In the 15th century their diversity is especially marked. The paintings of Hans Memling are rich in such designs; others are to be found among Baldovinetti, Ghirlandaio, Raffaelino del Garbo, Crivelli, Carpaccio, Foppa and numerous other contemporary artists. The most recent example known to us is shown in a portrait piece of the year 1560 by Sof. Anguissola in the Galerie Raczynski at Posen; here, however, the artist perhaps has made use of a rug which was already somewhat antique. Since in these paintings the design usually presents strikingly austere forms or (as among the Venetians, Carpaccio especially) has been but sketchily indicated to provide a picturesque effect, whereas the original pieces which are known to us exhibit a somewhat freer mode of treatment, it seems very likely that the artists have chosen certain models and have garbled them more or less to suit their purpose. This is the case especially with Jan van Eyck and his pupil Petrus Cristus, who smuggled Gothic motives into their versions; it is true as well for certain paintings of the Quattrocento, among others a little panel by Fra Angelico in the Academy at Florence, Piero della Francesca's altarpiece with Federico d'Urbino in the Brera, Baldovinetti's Madonna and his Annunciation in the Uffizi and a fresco of the year 1485 by Foppa in the Brera (Fig. 14). Thoroughly dependable by comparison are Holbein, whose fidelity in reproduction extends also to his Oriental rugs (for example in the painting of the ambassadors in the London National Gallery), Memling too at times, in whose Enthroned Madonnas the rug at Mary's feet is hardly ever absent, and Ghirlandaio (Fig. 15). The colors of this class are rich and striking; the key-note is usually either yellow or red. The borders are narrow and of elegant, angular design, derived either from inscriptions or from plant forms. Their small size made them extraordinarily suitable for artists' purposes and helps us to understand too just why the rugs of this class were used up so rapidly and so thoroughly.

An interesting combination of the two "Holbein" types is offered us by a carpet, strikingly larger than these others, from the Berlin Islamic Collection, in which the large rectangle-enclosed octagons are set about with little octagonal figures which in their turn contain stars; the three-part border provides the piece with an unusually rich frame (Fig. 16). Other examples on the same order (in the museum at Philadelphia among others) show some connection with Spanish and especially with Egyptian rugs of the last years of the 15th century, a type of weaving which quite certainly also found its way to Anatolia.

The third group must be included on ornamental grounds with the two that we have just discussed, despite many divergent features, and although Holbein himself seems to have made no use of them. In this type the octagonal figures, thoroughly broken up into geometric vines and arabesques, have been brought so close together that they can scarcely still be recognized for what they actually are. The style extends from the early 16th until deep into the 17th century and in its borders it suffers many transformations, but in respect to color it shows little change: in the field there is always a comely, bright red ground with yellow patterning (set off by several tones of blue and green); in the border a somewhat richer design occurs upon a blue or a green ground. Upon occasion gayer color contrasts are to be found, together with an approach to the Ushak types (see below). The smaller prayer rug size (Fig. 17) is the most frequently met with; nevertheless large pieces too are no rarity.

19. Turkish Arabesque Carpet (Lotto Rug)   *State Museums, Berlin*

The oldest paintings in which this scheme appears are works of the Venetian School: by Lorenzo Lotto, Girolamo dai Libri (in San Giorgio in Braida, about 1520, and in the Civic Museum at Verona, dated 1530), Luca Longhi (dated 1542, Fig. 18), in a portrait that ostensibly is of Cesare Borgia and is to be connected closely with Bronzino, which was transferred in 1819 from the Borghese Gallery to the collection of Baron Alphonse Rothschild (about 1535) and many others besides. It appears in remarkable abundance among later artists of the Netherlands, Flemish as well as Dutch. Jan Brueghel, Frans Francken, Cornelis de Vos, Simon de Vos, W. Key (dated

37

1543), Hendrik van Steenwyck and other Antwerp painters obviously possessed various rugs of this sort themselves. They are just as numerous in the works of G. Metsu, G. Terborch, Jan Steen, B. Fabritius, G. Bronckhorst, Nic. Maes, P. de Hooch, G. Schalcken and many other Hollanders. Then toward the close of the 17th century this class, which until a little while before had been so widespread, suddenly was to be seen no more in paintings. In the churches of Transylvania E. Schmutzler could still confirm in 1933 the existence of nearly a hundred original pieces, some of which have since that time found their way to market. In art and craft museums and in private homes, where they often are still in use as scatter rugs, there is no scarcity even of pieces in good preservation. Early examples as a rule share with the true "Holbein" rugs their characteristic interlaced-ribbon border (Fig. 19). Several specimens with the coats of arms of the allied Genoese families of Doria and Centurione knotted into their designs, in the Breslau and Hamburg Industrial Museums, and one recently acquired by J. V. McMullan (now in the Metropolitan Museum) furnish evidence that they occasionally were made up in the Orient to European order.

It can scarcely be doubted that all of the three species which we have just segregated were produced in one and the same district of Anatolia, although several different places may have been involved. Once again, more exact localization appears risky; in many a regard, relationships exist with the contemporary production of Ushak (see below), while on the other hand we can confirm an undeniable continuation of their motifs in later weavings which reportedly derived from the neighborhood of Bergama (the ancient Pergamum).

The Carpets of Ushak

The fabrication of carpets in Smyrna and its environs, one of the youngest industries of its kind in Asia Minor, presumably was established upon inducements and commissions from Europe, and has in part even been under European direct control. Notwithstanding this, it has indeed adhered the most strictly of any to the old designs and to the old technique. Characteristic of this manufacture are fat wool, loose knotting, high pile and a bland color scheme whereby its products may be distinguished from all other old carpets of the Orient. As a rule they are not elongated in shape but approach the square, a circumstance quite exceptional in Oriental weaving. Inasmuch as Smyrna carpets which are admirably proportioned to the rooms in which they lie have turned up both in Holland and in England most markedly in houses of the 18th century, it is quite unquestionable that such pieces were manufactured to order. Furthermore, the designs are not individualistic, but have been inspired by various ancient types, so we may strongly suspect that this industry was founded at or near Smyrna by the European (predominantly Dutch) colony which was flourishing there at the time, and that it was conducted to European order with Turkish weavers. This would account for their wide distribution in Europe, especially in Holland and England, together with their long success and their close adherence to the old traditions. On the other hand it would also explain the family likeness to the Smyrna weavings that is so apparent in the early products of the modern carpet industry when this was first founded in Europe.

Likewise to Smyrna, in view of their conformity of design, students formerly attempted to refer those ancient types which we are to take up next. This attribution may well be correct, provided that in assuming this we are not too narrow-minded about this localization, and think not too much in terms of the city itself but rather of the extensive hinterland for which Smyrna served as seaport. Aside from this, we still know today of a center of production in this district, namely Ushak, regarding which there were reports current even as early as the 16th century, and whose more recent products may easily be correlated with the old weavings. Hence it has been with some reason that the designation, "Ushak carpets", has been carried over from the later to the earlier group.

To this family belong, among the old examples, a variety of types which often differ among themselves in their designs, but can easily be perceived to be closely allied in both coloring and technique. Many of them show a characteristic medallion arrangement and call to mind by this, as well as by various peculiarities of their decor, certain Safavid designs which we are to consider later on. This correlation is most clearly apparent in one scheme which almost coincides with the basic layout of several groups of Persian carpets. In this the field displays an oval shield-like centerpiece of serrated outline with dainty attached motives, while the corners contain either portions of the central shield or else segments of large star forms. Now and then, especially in carpets of unusual extent, a part of the centerpiece (often a full half, cut off by the border) is repeated at each end. In this manner the decorative scheme of the field assumes the character of a portion cut from a pattern that we must think of as an infinite repeat in

20. Ushak Medallion Carpet *Formerly Count G. Stroganoff, Rome*

every direction, in antithesis to the centralized compositions which we find in Persian medallion carpets (cp. p. 87). The ornamentation of the shields presents a gay, richly entwining floral vine with stylized blossoms and leaves. A similar conception which, due to the total subordination and the slenderness of its scrolling stems, looks more like a patterning of scattered flowers fills the ground of the field. The border, edged by two narrow bands with ribbon-like patterning, as a rule displays a vine scroll with alternated leaves and flowers of rather loosely stylized form, or sometimes too the cloud bands with blossoms strewn between them. Quite rarely, in particularly early specimens, we still find the intertwined-letter designs. The arabesque occurs, large and handsomely formed, in the central medallion and in the cornerpieces. For the most part the colors are truly deep and forceful: the shield is normally brick-red, the border dark blue, the patterning in clear yellow, bright blue, green etc.

Carpets of this kind, which usually either are rather large or else are of very great size indeed, frequently come to light in the Orient itself; until not long ago they could be found in especial abundance in the churches of Italy; often too in those of Spain, Portugal, the Tyrol and South Germany. Thence through the art trade they have made their way into most of the greater museums of decorative arts and into many private homes. One of the most attractive examples in both coloring and design as well as among the oldest belonged to Count Gregor Stroganoff in Rome (Fig. 20); he acquired it in 1883 at the auction of the Castellani Collection. An admirably preserved and long-napped carpet of this sort nearly thirty feet in length was owned privately in Berlin some years ago; other magnificent specimens are or were in the Church of St. Michael at Munich, in the Chamber of Trade and Commerce at Bozen, in the Museum of Decorative Arts in Paris, in Count Dönhoff's collection, etc.

The time of origin of these carpets can be established approximately through their frequent appearances in old paintings of the most varied schools. We barely mention some of these which are of outstanding significance. A relatively early date is yielded us by a remarkable representation of the family of Henry VIII of England, which was painted at the inducement of Queen Elizabeth, about the year 1570 (displayed in the Tudor Exhibition in London in 1888, No. 158). Then we find a similar carpet in a Spanish picture, the great Zurbarán in the Louvre, which was done about 1622; we recognize an equivalent design in the portrait of the Princess Margareta Teresa by Velázquez in the Gallery at Vienna. Into the same period fall sundry Dutch paintings in which the same design occurs: the great Jan Vermeer in the Gallery at Dresden (dated 1656), "The Concert" by G. Terborch in the National Gallery in London and many others. In later pictures we will no longer find this class. Modifications to

41

the design as it is exhibited in typical representations over the course of nearly a century are scarcely noticeable: merely by greater simplicity, a more lucid disposition together with angularity of drawing in the leaves and flowers, especially those in the narrow guard stripes of the borders, can the earlier period be distinguished from the later. But then numerous carpets of this kind, which still may be seen in the mosques of Constantinople, Smyrna and their environs, right on down to the pieces which were manufactured until recently in the neighborhood of Ushak show the gradual deterioration of this variety; among these last only a faint residue of the vigorous style of the older rugs is still distinguishable.

21. Ushak Carpet with Coat of Arms
State Museums, Berlin

As an example of this great medallion scheme and its development, a carpet of moderate size in the Poldi Pezzoli Museum in Milan will interest us (see Viale, Pl. 158). Against the dark red ground rises in forcible contrast a great, angular black shield which, with its short ornamental pendants and the small black corner segments, preempts almost the entire field. The draftsmanship permits the Saracenic flower and arabesque to be divined only with difficulty, whereas in the border, at least, the palmette blossoms, which appear upon a black ground, have a fuller and more naturalistic form. In the capricious tendril-work which encompasses them one scarcely surmises its primary arrangement in oblong panels and swastika-rosettes. This hardening of all forms,

42

together with the rough character of the knotting, might allow us to infer that this must be a late adaptation of the design which is our subject. However, careful examination guides us toward the conclusion that we have here before us an ancient weaving which perhaps does not go back into the 16th century, as we suggested in former editions, but to the 17th certainly. On behalf of this presumption speak the antique patterning of the narrow guards, the technique, in no wise negligent, and above all the deep, bold coloring, with a preference for black and the excellent state of preservation of this color. — A comparatively late piece (of about 1700, no doubt) in the Berlin Museum commands attention because of the escutcheon of a Polish family (Wiesotowski?) which has been inserted in its design (Fig. 21); a companion piece is in the Wawel at Cracow.

Prisse d'Avennes (in "l'Art Arabe" III, Pl. 153) designates erroneously a remarkably fine early rug of this same class (and he gives a good colored illustration

22. Ushak Rug   *L. Bernheimer, Munich*

of it) as a work of the 18th century, yet at the same time he publishes another (Pl. 150), likewise shown in color, as a work of the 14th century, although the consanguinity of its design with that described above certainly makes such a variance in dating quite irrational. Inasmuch as this second kind also frequently appears in paintings, through these it can be established with certitude that this type was manufactured almost simultaneously with the first variety cited. This new design exhibits in its field an alternation of large eight-pointed stars of elegant form with smaller

43

four-pointed ones of similar configuration, and it is continuous in all directions like a section cut from an endless repeat. Now three, now five stars serve to fill up the length of the field in pieces of middling or of considerable size. Within their outlines the stars are adorned with a dainty, angular scrollwork of flowers and arabesques in attenuated form which is quite similar to that of the round central shields of the group last under discussion; just as in those, the ground of the field is covered with scattered blossoms on slender vines. Here too the border displays either the familiar cloud bands with the usual detached blossoms between these or else a floral festooning that forms a series of palmettes and is always firmly held in on either side by a narrow stripe with a ribbon-like stylized flowering vine (Fig. 22). The colors in this sort of carpet are even more stereotyped than in the last: the ground of the field indulges in a beautiful red (with its strewn blossoms in brownish or greenish tints); the stars have a deep blue ground with yellow patterning and the base color of the border is usually sky-blue.

In the possession of the Duke of Buccleuch are three such carpets whose cartouche borders are interrupted by the arms of Montagu; in one of these there is room enough for several large and small stars to lie side by side accross the breadth of the field (Fig. 23). They bear the dates 1584 and 1585 and through this circumstance they acquire notable historic value. It is readily apparent from characteristics of their technique that they were produced to English order in Ushak and not somewhere in England itself, as has occasionally been imagined. We can follow the emergence of this class in paintings from the middle of the 16th to the 17th century and do so in fact in all of the mainland countries that imported rugs from the Orient at that time. Among those paintings in which highly characteristic specimens occur, we will mention a celebrated picture by Paris Bordone, "The Ring", in the Academy at Venice, from the middle of the 16th century; here the throne of the doges stands upon a superb carpet of the class. From the year 1614 dates a large portrait by Marcus Geeraerts, who was active in England at the time, and this includes a similar example; its equal lies upon the floor in a painting done perhaps twenty years later by Zurbarán, which is in the Raczynski Gallery in Posen. These carpets used to appear from time to time in the Italian rug trade; an example of remarkable loveliness in both coloring and design is the property of the Church of St. Anne in Augsburg, a large specimen in admirable preservation belongs

44

to Count Dönhoff, still others to the Austrian Museum, the Musée des Arts Décoratifs, the Philadelphia Museum, the Museum of Industrial Art in Copenhagen, the Metropolitan Museum (from J. V. McMullan's collection), to L. Bernheimer, etc.

23. Ushak Carpet with Coat of Arms (1584)   *The Duke of Buccleuch, England*

This type, when it has not as yet been completely perfected, displays a more unusual design in which the stars of the field still have not adopted an altogether regular and stable form and their inner patterning has not assumed the rigid, dry construction which we find in the later pieces, but ordinarily discloses full, handsome palmette-blossoms which, in a more relaxed treatment, take charge in the border as well (see 3rd edition, Fig. 70). The ground is a dark cherry-red, the stars have a dark blue. The drawing and stylization place this exceptional variety at the outset of the 16th century. Another design equally rare in incidence is closely connected with all of the three schemes which we have mentioned; its arrangement is the same as one, it has drawing in common with the second, with the third it shares certain peculiar details. This design likewise we must refer to the

24. Ushak Medallion Carpet   *L. Bernheimer, Munich*

16th century. On a deep blue ground with the customary vine scroll (in a
yellow hue) lie three or five medallions of like size, fashioned as oblong
hexagons and grounded in red; between these, resting against the border
on both sides, are half-stars with bright blue grounds, and all of these
figures have tiny pendant projections. The decor of flowers and arabesques

46

and their manner of stylization find counterparts now here, now there among the major groups, and so do the coloring and the decorative scheme of the border. A choice example of this kind, apart from those in the Austrian Museum, which formerly belonged to Baron H. von Tucher, is now owned by L. Bernheimer in Munich (Fig. 24).

25. Ushak Rug   *Formerly A. Cassirer, Berlin*

A divergent motif, of which indeed only one example is known (3rd ed., Fig. 74, destroyed in the war), but which is of peculiar significance in view of its earlier connotations as well as its influence upon future periods, shows the same scheme as the second group, but this time in a tighter arrangement. From one star to another on both sides angular tendrils with sparse leaves and blossoms are led in such a fashion that these large stellate flowers — for of course that is what they amount to — stand in a sort of a rhomboidal lattice. The border displays the cloud band, with blossoms scattered in between, precisely as in other pieces with which the rich, brilliant coloring also corresponds. The ground of the field, as occurs quite rarely among these pieces, is a deep blue; the basic color of the border and of the large starlike flowers is cinnabar red; the general decor introduces a bright yellow, two greens, bright blue, salmon-red and white. From this the provenance of this rug can be taken with assurance to be the same district to which the other varieties belong, and the time of its origin would likewise be about the same. Ever since the 17th century this Ushak variant has been copied by preference in "Smyrna carpets" destined for Europe.

Upon occasion quite dissimilar examples also occur which repeat a single motive (palmette-buds, cloud bands, lanceolate leaves or the like) over the entire field in unvaried rows, yet their palette and their border

patterns always demonstrate their membership in the great Ushak family. They are to be seen for the first in the latter part of the 17th century (Fig. 25).

In affiliation with the Ushak groups which we have just described there arose also several types of prayer rugs, whose purpose enjoined small dimensions and accordingly led to mere selection from the treasury of forms which had been developed in designs of greater scale. One of the most frequently repeated motifs of this kind, in which for the sake of symmetry the prayer arch has been provided at both ends, has been likewise attested for us by paintings over the course of nearly a century and original

26. Ushak Prayer Rug
Metropolitan Museum, New York

pieces handled in this manner were by no means scarce a while ago in the Italian art trade (Fig. 26). The field presents upon a monochrome ground one small four- or six-pointed star, a severely stylized hanging lamp in the head of the niche, and spandrel ornaments which can still be recognized by an observant eye as capricious cloud bands. The border either has the same motif, with blossoms scattered in between, or a loose sort of a palmetted festooning of flowers and leaves. Sometimes the arabesque too appears as a decorative element, in quite the same way as in the larger designs which we have mentioned previously. As a rule the usual pair of guard stripes are present, but frequently still more of these are

Ushak Prayer Rug   State Museums, Berlin

added. The colors are very deep and bright: a forceful red in the field, set
off by a deep blue as the principal border color; the spandrels are usually
deep green, the patternings in the stars and in the borders as well are
varicolored. Original pieces of this kind still appear, aside from those in
museums, quite frequently in
private collections, and in
paintings from the middle of the
16th century on; as in a double
portrait of Queen Mary and
Henry VII at Althorp (about
1550 to 1560), in a portrait from
the brush of Francesco Vene-
ziano in 1561 (formerly in the
possession of Mr. Holford,
Westonbirt), in several paintings
by Tintoretto (for example in
the Brera at Milan), in a painting
by Matteo Rosselli in the
Academy at Florence, about
1620, etc. After this time,
however, they are to be found
no more.

27. Ushak Prayer Rug
Musée des Arts Décoratifs, Paris

Even so, we still possess
several examples, rare though
these may be, which certify that
at a much earlier date than this
the mihrab type of design had
led to characteristic and novel
conformations. In this connection to be sure we can name but one piece, yet
this one is all the more conclusive: that rug, owned formerly by Herr von
Angeli in Vienna and at present domiciled in the Berlin Museum, superb in
its coloring, with a great cloud band which fills the entire lower part of the
field with its grandiose pattern, enclosing there one magnificiently stylized
and fully Saracenic blossom (Pl. II). Aside from the archaic draftsmanship of
the principal elements, as well as of the smaller incidental details, and,
above all, that of the severe arabesques in the spandrels, the harmonious
colors are well adapted to a key-note of deep blue and the extremely

narrow double border is quite characteristic of an early origin. The knotting is rather coarse, but this fact cannot soften the impressive effect of truly consummate artistic execution. In age this paragon must be placed ahead of all other Ushak prayer rugs; that it belongs to this category is proved not only by its characteristic scale of colors, but also by a whole series of

28. Ushak Rug with Rows of Niches   *Formerly Haim, London*

examples which ring the changes in counterplay of cloud band and niche, often in quite stiffened forms, from century to century and yet belong unmistakably within the Ushak classification (Fig. 27). These occur upon occasion even in paintings of the 16th century (Dosso Dossi, F. Floris, etc.). In conclusion it should be mentioned additionally that in Ushak since the 16th century — and later on in Smyrna, too — carpets wrongly spoken of as "family prayer rugs" have been produced, which are furnished with rows of individual niches and which have enjoyed especial favor as floor pieces in mosques; in Istanbul they may still be encountered in many places of worship. Often a lamp hangs down from the arch of each mihrab and the places which are to be occupied by the feet of the worshipers are set out ornamentally upon the ground of every niche (Fig. 28).

50

Other Rugs of the 16th and 17th Centuries

In some distinct district of Asia Minor there was developed a species of rug which it is difficult to classify, yet which is closely akin to the Ushaks in many of its peculiar features. Such pieces used to appear rather frequently in Italian trade some time ago and occasionally too in South Germany and in Turkey. Here the basic color is white (or more rarely a creamy yellow) and the field offers no elaborate composition, but simply archaic floral forms, frozen in a singular manner into mathematical regularity and repeated row after row, textile fashion. This design (Fig. 29) is comprised

29. So-called "Bird Rug"   *Formerly F. Werner, Berlin*

of rhomboid leaf-motives (which have been interpreted as birds that face in two directions, but which actually derive from a vegetal source) in regular alignment between rosettes and scattered flowers. Its time of origin is provided for us through its incidence in paintings by Varotari in the gallery of the Hermitage (about 1625) and in the art trade (Fig. 30), as well as in a painted ceiling by Peter Candid in the Royal Palace at Munich (1587); accordingly we will fix the fabrication of this type at some time between the middle of the 16th and the middle of the 17th century. As support for this decision we have the insertion of the arms of an archbishop of Lemberg

(1614—1630) into the design of one of these so-called "bird rugs" and the date 1646 on another which is in the church at Schaessburg (Transylvania). The border shows either the cloud band — quite in the Ushak manner — between attenuated vines with scattered flowers, or else a characteristic

30. Detail from a Painting by Varotari
Berlin Art Market, 1927

arrangement of reciprocal triangles in which perfectly rigid palmettes can be identified between misshapen arabesques.

This identical border is also commonly found with a field design which displays in uniform repetition three diminutive balls, placed one above the others, over a pair of narrow ribbons, and these are spread as a motif over the entire surface in a disposition which conforms again to the normal artistic treatment of textiles. As with the class just described, this too ordinarily has a white

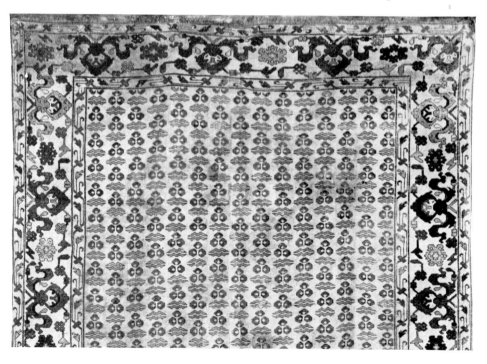

31. Carpet with White Field   *Bardini Museum, Florence*

ground and the patterning is in rich and brilliant colors. This motif of "globes and lightning" or "clouds and moons" — in actuality a heraldic recall of the tiger and leopard skins worn by one-time rulers (see p. 173) — is to be found, with complete analogy, in Turkish brocades and tiles of the 16th—17th centuries, so that the dating assumed heretofore appears to be conclusive for both varieties.

Rugs of this kind, for the most part of large size, are owned by the National Museum and the Bardini Museum in Florence (Fig. 31), the Philadelphia and the Metropolitan Museums, as also the museums at Istanbul and Konia, among others. Smaller pieces too from time to time occur in either pattern, sometimes with a niche incorporated (Fig. 32), and they persist in rather degenerate drawing well into the 18th century. An interesting specimen in the Bavarian Nat. Museum (Fig. 33) is closely connected to the class

32. Prayer Rug with White Field
Art Institute, Chicago

through its white field and the previously mentioned three-cornered palmettes in its border. Its spandrels are filled with an oblique and irregular scrollwork.

The so-called "Siebenbürger rugs" constitute a more extensive group which, however, first came into fashion in the 17th century. They owe this title to the circumstance that in the churches of Siebenbürgen (Transylvania) they serve in quite considerable numbers — in 1933 there still were 113 of

53

them — as endowment, and so were mistakenly regarded as the products of this area. Their Anatolian extraction is beyond question and it seems that for certain definite reasons these particular weavings, which became well-known under Turkish overlordship, straightway came to enjoy especial favor in Transylvania, not exclusively, however, but merely to a more marked degree than was the case with other classes of Anatolian rugs. That these pieces were manufactured expressly to order from that district is quite contrary to the facts, for they can be pointed out in many Dutch paintings, and were widely distributed over the remainder of Europe as well.

33. Prayer Rug with White Field
National Museum, Munich

All of the pieces which are included in this group have the form of prayer rugs, but are rather large in size for the purpose and for the most part have arches at both ends of the field, as do certain types of Ushaks. Here, however, we do not find one central star in brave isolation against a bare field, but vase-like hanging lamps introduced into the arches, with the balance of the surface filled up with leaf and blossom work on slender stems. The spandrels either have stiff arabesques or else geometric floral rosettes and lanceolate leaves. The easiest way to recognize the class is by their individualistic border, which almost invariably is composed of oblong cartouches bearing pairs of arabesques, in alternation with eight-pointed stars that contain rosettes, or often, too, of only one of these motifs repeated. More rarely, palmette-trails or cloud bands have been substituted. As a rule the guards have the well-known "reciprocal fleur-de-lis" design (Fig. 34) or, now and then, rows of little rosettes.

The color tones are pure and bright against a red, yellow or blue background, with some contrasting hue in the spandrels and a harmonious counterchange in the border. In later examples the lamps tend to be replaced by great floral palmettes or else the whole of the field's ornamentation is often gathered up together to produce a centerpiece (Fig. 35). Subject to such trends as these the class passes over in the 18th century into that rug classification which is expressed in the trade as "Milas" (or "Melez"), and in this guise — usually with a red field — it can be followed throughout the entire 19th century; in Transylvania we can verify this through bequest dates of 1710, 1718, 1719, 1752.

34. So-called Transylvanian Rug
Industrial Museum, Budapest

The rugs which have been preserved in Transylvania itself — including some with white fields and others with the arabesque-vine design of the so-called Holbein carpets, too — have been brought together by E. Schmutzler in a publication of their own, with many interesting individual features. In earlier days typical "Siebenbürger" rugs appeared also in Hungarian, Polish, Italian and South German churches, from which, through the trade, they eventually reached European and American museums and private collections. The Budapest Museum of Arts and Crafts owns a magnificent series — and there are seven pieces in Skokloster (Sweden) that probably came from the estate of Count K. G. Wrangel, who brought them with him from the Orient in 1653, so that at this point we must plead for a more elastic *terminus ante quem* for this class. It has been frequently reproduced with great accuracy by various Dutch artists of the 17th century, such as Th. de Keyzer, C. de Vos, P. Codde, C. Netscher, J. Verkolje, C. van Man, J. v. d. Merck etc., and in exceptional instances by the later Italians, such as B. Castiglione, too. It still appears in the 18th century in a painting by Jak. van Schuppen (Vienna Gallery), in another one by P. Batoni in the Hermitage and in the large portrait of the Empress Maria Theresa in the Belvedere at Vienna.

35. So-called Transylvanian Rug
Dr. S. Lutomirski, Milan

Localization of these rugs is not easy; in many respects there exists a loose relationship with the Ushaks, which, however, is not sufficient to cause us to search in this district for the place where they would actually have been produced. It must be that we are dealing with a center whose exportations went out primarily to the European provinces of the Ottoman realm. Whether we really can consider Milas in southwest Asia Minor as the center in question, as has been claimed by the trade for the later varieties, cannot be decided out of hand.

Upon better evidence Ladik (probably the ancient Laodicea in western Anatolia) is identified as the place of origin of a class in which we can certify the continuity of an individual decorative style from the classical

36. So-called Column-Ladik Rug   *Formerly in the Davanzati Palace, Florence*

57

period on down into the late 19th century. Its older products exalt themselves beyond all others within the periphery of Anatolian rugs through this peculiarity, that although they are intended as prayer rugs their central feature does not consist of one niche alone, but, as a likely

37. Anatolian Prayer Rug (Fragment)   *State Museums, Berlin*

development of the mihrab idea, an architectural treatment based upon the ogive tripled through the use of columns. Almost as a set rule the ground is red and is crowned by a row of the crenellated forms that we usually speak of as "vandykes", above which rise strongly stylized tulip-stalks. The border is set with medallion-like lobed octagons which contain shrubby ornamentation. The guards, which often differ from each other in pattern, have undulating leaf or blossom work (Fig. 36). In the 18th century the trisection is simplified and eventually, through the use of plain separating bars, detached from its pillared supports. In many cases too it has been wholly abandoned so that frequently a field is formed which appears quite narrow and constricted in proportion to the border. However, the crenellation-like motif of vandykes and tulip-stems is maintained until well into the 19th century, whereas deviations from the classic pattern are to be noted in the borders.

Good examples of the typical "Column-Ladiks" dating back as far as the 17th century are in the Budapest Museum of Arts and Crafts, in the Metropolitan Museum, in the Textile Museum in Washington, in other public collections and in private hands. It is highly probable that the idea of trisection did not originate in Ladik itself, but was introduced into Anatolia by Egyptian masters with their motif of the niche's arch resting upon columns (Fig. 53).

The other kinds of Asia Minor prayer rugs familiar to the trade, which still today rejoice in greater popularity as merchandise for use: the Ghiordes, Kulahs, Mudjurs, the Kirshehrs and many others, even if they have been influenced by classic designs, did not receive their characteristic stamp before the 18th century and consequently do not fall within the scope of our manual. Many of them do hark back to extraordinarily rare and ancient prototypes (see Fig. 37).

RUGS OF THE CAUCASUS

In our attempts to single out works of earlier epochs to which we can trace back later phases of development, or when we cast about among our stock for really ancient knotted rugs, we find ourselves in the greatest of dilemmas. To be sure we have a series of Asia Minor, Egyptian and Spanish pieces which we can date back to the 15th century with conviction and a certain few examples which may be assigned to an era even earlier. Aside from these, however, there is but one group that can be taken into account in this sense which can be delimited with any degree of precision: that of the so-called "Armenian dragon rugs".

None too many weavings of this kind have been handed down to us and in paintings too they are extremely difficult to authenticate. In fact the first mention of this class was made in the first edition of this book; in the Munich Exhibition it was represented to the extent of a half-dozen pieces and by 1948, when a special showing of such specimens as were owned in America was arranged by the Textile Museum in Washington, about thirty pieces were available for display.

In this type we find conjoined in an ascending diamond or lozenge trelliswork a series of dissimilar panels in which, aside from floral motives which we encounter in orderly repetition, a single animal has been depicted in each panel, or else two like animals face to face. These creatures are strongly stylized and now and then they are drawn so rigidly that they are scarcely to be recognized as animals at all, or is their species to be determined. They are set off in strong coloristic contrast against a monochrome and unpatterned ground into which, at most, a few isolated little angular blossoms or other ornamental space-fillers may have been introduced. Instead of a wide border treatment we find here merely a narrow stripe with simple, severely formalized vine scrolls, or else floral or leaf ornament; usually the enhancement of these borders by means of guard stripes both without and within is lacking, too. The individual panels or lozenges are separated from each other by bands of highly geometric, stiff lancet leaves. The colors are bold primary tones; the background will in most cases be red, blue or dark brown. The material is rough wool, with a high nap and solid Anatolian knotting.

All these attributes lend to these pieces an extraordinarily austere and primitive, and at times even barbaric character, yet one that is at root extremely consistent and stylistic. Hence we may at once dismiss the assumption that they represent merely a barbarization of the animal carpets which were developed in Persia in the 16th century (see below). To the contrary, one might be tempted to overestimate the time interval that separates these weavings from those of the heyday of the Safavids and to envision a gulf yawning between the two. F. R. Martin was led astray by this view, in accord with which he takes the rugs that we are discussing all the way back into the 13th century. Surely they are not as old as this; for despite every difference of style they invariably show certain primary relationships with the vase carpets of the 16th century (see below, p. 139). These include floral motives that are analogous, borders that for the most part are narrow, and, at times, a fully parallel apportionment of the field. The "dragon rugs" owe their archaic appearance to a very consistently executed stylistic purpose: every ornamental motive has been denaturalized and translated, as it were, into an idiom suitable to carpets that are to be knotted more coarsely. In this respect, certainly, they resemble the Anatolian animal rugs which we have touched on previously, but they differ from these, however, in basic composition although both types conform to a "progressive" arrangement: that is, they were intended to be seen from one direction only.

Here certainly we are not faced with the productions of some manufactory, but with the fruits of a highly-developed folk-art which in the existing examples at our disposal we find either at full maturity or else on the road to decline; their early history is unknown to us. Of course there has been some contact with alien art elements. This follows from their frequent use of Far Eastern fabulous animals (besides the dragon, especially favored, also the phoenix, kylin, fohu etc.) which, moreover, were not merely stylized in a heraldic manner, like the rest of the animals, but usually were imitated with little understanding. As regards floral designs, palmette forms of various kinds predominate, sometimes as candelabra-like structures; several forms of rosettes appear as well, together with rather tiny leaf and blossom elements on short stems.

38. So-called Dragon Rug   *State Museums, Berlin*

The most important and ancient example of the entire class, nearly 23 feet in length, from the collection of Th. Graf, was presented by W. v. Bode to the Islamic Department in Berlin in 1905. On a blue field laid out with a yellow and red lozenge diaper it displays in most of its panels, in symmetrical arrangement and repeated at considerable intervals, heavily

62

39. So-called Dragon Rug   *Formerly A. Cassirer, Berlin*

outlined animal figures sometimes singly, sometimes in pairs confronted
— dragons, kylins, stags, bulls, lions or leopards, hares and the like —
parted in some cases by leafy shrubs or cypresses (Fig. 38). This carpet,
which was partially destroyed by an air attack in 1945, survives only as a
rather large fragment, including, however, every important element. It is

40. So-called Dragon Rug   *Textile Museum, Washington*

said to have been acquired in Damascus; the assertion that it came from a
mosque there can hardly have been correct, for that would mean that
nobody had recognized its animal motives as such, and that for that reason
it was not found objectionable for use in a religious place.

Several other examples, which now are for the most part in American
collections, came to light in Italian churches; notwithstanding their
correspondence in basic scheme they display many an individuality,
especially in their borders. These, however (see Fig. 39), may well be
several decades younger, as one might venture to conclude from their
comparative paucity of motives and from other stylistic touches. A piece

in the Textile Museum in Washington offers us an interesting bit of documentation for, in addition to the name of the owner or of the person who commissioned it, Husayn Beg, it bears also the date "Muharram 1001" (October, 1592, Fig. 40; the reading proposed by others, of A. H. 1101, i. e. 1689 A. D., is not convincing and provides an improbably late dating). Its arrangement is clearer and the animals are more plainly recognizable, but when we compare it with the carpet from the Graf Collection, the impoverishment of its border as well as of its field is so obvious that we can without hesitation assign to the rug first mentioned a date almost a century earlier, that is about 1500. It is possible that the rug with a lattice design (Fig. 41) which is portrayed in Piero Pollaiuolo's Annunciation in Berlin, about 1480, belongs to this class, even though animal figures are not distinguishable in its panels. Farther back than this we do not venture to go with this entire group, but at all events there exists a basis for assumption that the existing specimens originated for the most part in the course of the 16th century.

41. Detail from a Painting by P. Pollaiuolo
Gemäldegalerie, Berlin

Later the palmette forms gain the upper hand, and aside from these as field decoration only the dragons appear, more distorted and dismembered than ever (Fig. 42), until in the 18th century these too ultimately will vanish.

When we come to the localization of the "dragon rugs", the fact that Armenian inscriptions occur in certain of them, together with the actual mention of "Armenian" carpets by medieval authorities, has led to the postulation that in these rugs we are actually dealing with the products of the Armenian people. This thesis has been energetically defended over and over again on the part of Armenian authors. To the contrary it is refuted not only by the confirmation of a text (we have just mentioned it) which is thoroughly Moslem in style, but also by the unmistakably Islamic character of the decorative scheme. If these rugs, as has occasionally been suggested,

42. So-called Dragon Rug (destroyed)   *State Museums, Berlin*

actually served as floor-pieces in the Christian churches of Armenia, why is it then that in not a single one of them has there been preserved any allusion to such a religious purpose? The most plausible answer to the questions which have been raised concerning this class still is that in these

66

we are dealing with weavings from Transcaucasia which have been worked out within the scope of the same factors which have always determined the course of the knotting art in the Near East, be the weavers Christian or Mohammedan. The technique may well have been disseminated as a home industry through the Caucasus area quite early by Turkish tribes and practiced also by Armenians from time to time, without their having been able to influence the stylistic trend. However, whether knotted rugs were specifically meant by the "Armenian carpets" of some Early Medieval sources is more than questionable; it is much more likely that by this expression were signified the products of the many older weaving methods which have proved outstandingly successful in this very Armeno-Caucasian region, and among which individual techniques such as the Sumak and the Silé had perhaps already been perfected many centuries before. A more precise delimitation of the neighborhood in which these "dragon carpets" originated is not possible at this time; reminiscences of their classical phase survive in various categories of Caucasian

43. Caucasian Rug (fragment) *State Museums, Berlin*

weavings (Kazak, Kuba, Sumak etc.) until well into the 19th century and can be pointed out also in the embroideries of this region, which closely resemble the carpets.

In the 16th century a type of rug must already have been worked out — presumably in a different center of production — which, renouncing all forms of animal decoration, organizes its field into a trellis of large-scale diamonds set with glorious palmettes. Each diamond panel in its turn contains a severely stylized flower of chalice form between a pair of lanceolate leaves. A smaller-scale, allover sprinkling of blossoms and rosettes of various kinds is deployed along a second and underlying finely-drawn network of lozenges. An imposing fragment of this school, blue of ground, with an attractive border of reciprocal leafage, is in the Islamic Section of the Berlin Museum (Fig. 43), another one in the Victoria & Albert Museum.

The stamp of a relatively early origin is shown by still another class of Caucasian carpets, which is quite unlike the other weavings of the land, yet in many respects must be considered to be closely allied to the type first mentioned. The field is adorned with rows of T-shaped polygonal shields or cartouches, alternately turned top to bottom, and between these rows are interpolated chains of octofoils of two different types. Both motives are filled with palmettes and other sharply stylized floral designs. Branches with stout stems occupy the background spaces and are thickly garnished with almond-like blossoms in the first band of interstices, in the next with fruits on the order of pomegranates, foliage in the third. A complete example in the Philadelphia Museum (formerly in the McIlhenny Collection) has a border which is strongly suggestive of the dragon carpets of the 16th century, a second was in the Lamm Collection (Fig. 44), with a stiff border of arabesques and palmettes that displays relationships with adjacent Northwest Persia; J. V. McMullan in New York has recently acquired a third. The Berlin Museum and other collections possess good-sized fragments of these strikingly-colored weavings which otherwise are so extremely elusive. A later variant, with greatly reduced medallions and Persian elements in both field and border, is in the Metropolitan Museum in New York.

Now and then we will encounter transitional pieces and individualistic modifications of the classic Caucasian types last mentioned. Thus a very large rug from the mosque at Nigde (Asia Minor) and a rug of Prince Sanguszko's which has also survived intact exhibit exactly the same palmette-adorned lozenge system as the Berlin fragment (Fig. 43), but show in the panels only large quadrilateral figures with palmette-blossoms, and not the severely formalized chalice-flowers (lilies?). These last appear by themselves, conversely, arranged as a constantly repeated leitmotiv, with

44. Caucasian Floral Rug   *Formerly the Late Mr. Lamm, Näsby*

handsome color contrasts, in other knotted weavings of the same region, which in some cases may date back as far as the 17th century. In conclusion, we still must mention a rug in the Austrian Museum, whose red field is filled with palmettes, rosettes and chalice-blossoms in accordance with the classic Caucasian formula, but here they have been freed from their latticed prison cells (Sarre-Trenkwald I, Pl. 40).

69

EGYPTIAN CARPETS

Among the Oriental rugs of the classical period there is one category which has long been the cause of much disagreement, since it stands in complete isolation from all others. For this reason it has indeed been attributed to the most diverse regions of the Islamic world. In the last few decades searching investigations have made it increasingly plain for the first time that its homeland is not to be sought anywhere in Asia, but in Egypt, where a carpet industry must have been flourishing at least as long ago as the 15th century. It is perfectly true that fragments of carpet have come to light in the course of excavations in Fostât (Old Cairo) which go back to the first centuries of Islamic chronology. In these, however, no true rug-knotting is involved, but weaving in a looping technique which was developed to a very high level in the Nile Valley. In this method the loops, when cut open, produce a fleecy piled surface that often is deceptively similar to that of the knotted Oriental rug.

Among the products of the 15th to the 17th centuries which claim our attention now, we will distinguish three groups that can be clearly differentiated on the basis of design and, to a degree too, through other details characteristic of the weave. The oldest, that of the Mamluk rugs, thrived over a period of somewhat longer duration than the sultanate after which it has been christened (to 1517). This group is remarkable for its very restrained palette, which in most instances is restricted to a cherry-red that customarily is dominant, a bright green and a pure, but never deep, blue; to these are occasionally added some yellow and one additional color tone or another, employed most discreetly. The material is sheep's wool of a peculiar luster; it allows soft light reflections which were effectively blended through the nature of the design. As a rule this consists of geometric structures which appear to have been thrown together quite haphazardly, but which in reality were very well ordered, together with small and varied, stylized botanical forms. The center presents an elaborately detailed octagon or else a large star whose construction is equally complex;

in pieces of great size several of these elements lie side by side. Transverse friezes with a separate patterning usually are introduced above and below these centerpieces. The border, which is never contrasted with the field in

45. Mamluk Carpet *Austrian Museum of Applied Arts, Vienna*

color as in other classes, frequently displays an alternation of octofoils or circular rosettes and oblong cartouches with varied internal ornament.

Original pieces of this kind still come to hand in comparatively respectable numbers. Formerly they could be seen in Italian churches and, sporadically, in those of South Germany also, often of course in sorry condition due to the fragility of the materials, which would not brook a century-long utilization as floor coverings. They then were passed on through the trade to public and private collections. Among specimens which still are well-preserved we can mention several in the Islamic

Section in Berlin and in the Austrian Museum (Fig. 45), and most emphatically a stately series in the Textile Museum in Washington. A singularly majestic example, nearly 30 feet in length and rather narrow,

46. Mamluk Carpet *Formerly Simonetti Gallery, Rome*

was once owned by the antiquary Simonetti in Rome. It had an intricate stepped arrangement of geometric figures (Fig. 46). Smaller sizes (Fig. 47) present new variations with each example. For beauty they are all excelled by the unique palace carpet executed in silk, a part of the court treasures

Cairene Ottoman Rug   *State Museums, Berlin*

47. Mamluk Rug

Art Museum, Philadelphia

48. Mamluk Carpet in Silk   *Austrian Museum of Applied Arts, Vienna*

of the Hapsburgs, which is now in the Austrian Museum of Applied Arts. A matchless and wondrous achievement of Oriental industry, it can truly be characterized as a kaleidoscope translated into textile form (Fig. 48). It intrigues us much less for the multitude of ornamental forms employed in it than for the fabulous ingenuity with which these have been organized into constantly interchanging combinations.

These rugs are seldom found in ancient paintings, perhaps because their decor seemed too unimpressive, and when they do occur are often merely suggested. Their employment is exclusive to artists of the Venetian School, if we take this in its broadest sense, as by Marco Marziale, Vittore Carpaccio, Giovanni Bellini, Lorenzo Lotto, Bonifazio Veronese, G. B. Moroni and others. Moretto's frescoes in the Palazzo Salvadego at Brescia, with likenesses of ladies of the House of Martinengo, are estimated as particularly important evidence of this kind. In at least six instances Mamluk rugs, very accurately depicted, are shown hanging over parapets, and these pieces surely must have been decades older than the paintings, which were actually executed around 1530. It has been taken for granted that such carpets as these must have been meant by the "tappeti damaschini" which were frequently mentioned in inventories of Venetian families taken during the 15th and 16th centuries. From this designation it was concluded that they originated in Syria. Yet as a matter of fact a rug industry has never existed in that country, so no doubt we should interpret the Venetian labelling more correctly as suggesting that by this term were to be understood not the products of Damascus itself, but rugs which were ornamented — because of their peculiar effect — damask-fashion. Still today they frequently appear both in literature and in the trade as "Damascus carpets".

Their ascription to Egypt is now so firmly established that we have no need at this time to rehearse one by one the several arguments which have been advanced for this view. Kurt Erdmann has carefully compiled them in a specific treatise in 1938, and further investigations, such as a study of the employment of Pharaonic papyrus-umbels, have confirmed anew the correctness of this theory. There is documentary verification for the production of carpets in Cairo, at least since 1474 when it was mentioned in G. Barbaro's account of his travels; just how far back it actually does extend cannot yet be determined. Yet surely the majority of the existing examples whose decorative scheme corresponds to the Mamluk tradition must be referred to the 15th century, and it is scarcely to be supposed that the class could have survived the first third of the 16th. For shortly after its conquest by the Osmanli Turks (1517) a change of style set in in Egypt which, due to the establishment of a manufactory working for the court in Istanbul, found a particularly strong expression in the carpet industry.

49. Cairene Ottoman Carpet (destroyed)   *Formerly State Museums, Berlin*

The Cairene Ottoman rugs correspond with those of the previous period both in material and in color range, and the palette is extended only through the more plentiful use of yellow, white and a few other tints; occasionally, however, they were inclined to be satisfied with the three Cairene basic colors. Nevertheless, if there have been doubts expressed regarding the continuity of their production, these were based entirely upon the fact that the new rugs renounced completely the decorative orientation which had been observed up to that point. Vegetation which at

50. Cairene Ottoman Rug   *Musée des Arts Décoratifs, Paris*

times is naturalistic, at times stylized in a peculiar manner, is deployed luxuriantly and, in forms that are known to us from Turkish wall tiles and brocades, quite fills the field in endless continuation, interrupted by a large or a small medallion, quadrants of which are often repeated in the corners. Carnations, tulips, hyacinths, lilies, peonies and other flowers, together

51. Cairene Ottoman Prayer Rug   *State Museums, Berlin*

with gracefully sweeping lancet leaves, sumptuous palmettes and delicate sprays of blossoms, constitute the rich flora of these carpets (Figs. 49, 50), whose borders charm the eye with their elegant solutions for the corner problem, while in the guard stripes almost invariably little rosette-flowers appear all in a row. It is merely by way of exception that we will still find appropriations levied upon the Mamluk tradition, while, on the other hand, the coming revolution in decor is already heralded in a few specimens which we still count as belonging to the earlier group.

In a pure folk-art such a radical overturn would be quite inconceivable, but then in the operation of a manufactory the introduction of a completely novel program can be accomplished with a minimum of confusion. With this change of orientation, it was significant that the idea of a governing medallion, even if with a different conception, had already been put to use

78

and therefore was not stimulated first by foreign — e. g. Persian — models, as we might otherwise have imagined. The circumstance that color contrasts between field and border were still eschewed as far as might be possible is further evidence of this independence of origin. Only in the prayer rugs, particularly charming in their own fashion and extraordinarily diverse in their artistry, which issued from the same workshops does this alien influence occasionally stand out more sharply, (see Fig. 51 and Pl. III). We possess a detailed report of the activities of the Cairo manufactory from the French traveler Thévenot in the year 1663; it was still in full operation at that time.

When in French, Italian, Spanish and also in German inventories of the 16th and 17th centuries rugs are mentioned from time to time, which are accredited to Cairo in a more or less garbled orthography ("Cairin", "Querin", "Cagiarin", "alkheirisch"), doubtless the reference is to the Egypto-Ottoman group. Often especial attention is called to the fact that one of them is a "table-rug", and such covers are occasionally still to be met with among the relatively numerous original pieces which yet exist (in cross-form at San Gimignano and in the Victoria & Albert Museum, circular in the Corcoran Gallery, Washington). Moreover, pieces of notable size occur too; frequently, of course, in a worn-out condition. In paintings this class appears but rarely; other than a few Hollanders (G. Flinck, P. de Hooch, H. Sorgh), several 17th century Spanish painters (Pereda, Pareja) seem to have owned them.

How greatly these Egyptian products were prized at the court at Constantinople is apparent from this fact, among others, that in the year 1585 the sultan ordered that a number of master weavers together with a quantity of their rug materials be brought to his capital from Cairo. From the imperial workshop under their superintendence, established perhaps at Brussa, may have emerged a group of weavings which constantly exhibit silk warping, cotton for white areas in place of wool, more intense coloring, and in their designs, in which the Cairene style was otherwise carefully maintained, certain details such as cloud bands which were not in general use in Egypt. One of the most beautiful specimens of this school, with an individualistic scheme of round medallions, rosettes, blossomwork, tiger stripes etc., in amazingly fine knotting (325 knots to the square inch) used to be in the Islamic Section in Berlin (Fig. 52). Many of these rugs are wholly of silk, too, the prayer rugs customarily having a gleaming red and

79

unpatterned mihrab. These pieces have influenced to a high degree the various types of Anatolian prayer rugs which became important after about 1700, particularly the Ghiordes and the Ladiks; the "column scheme" so characteristic of the latter (see p. 58) was foreshadowed by rugs with architecturally organized fields which form a part of the group now dealt

52. Egypto-Ottoman Rug (destroyed)   *Formerly State Museums, Berlin*

with (Fig. 53). Such contrasts will serve to clarify the comparative coarseness of the Anatolian varieties (see Fig. 36).

We still must make some brief mention of a third class, whose relationship to Egypt is beyond question, yet which, through certain individual characteristics, is set somewhat apart from both of the others. Eight-pointed stars, centered by little crosses and enclosed by diminutive cypresses, are set in hexagons or octagons which, built out into squares by ornamented spandrels, are repeated in rows throughout the field. Medallion structures are not in evidence, but the basic scheme is unmistakably

53. Egypto-Ottoman "Column" Rug   *Metropolitan Museum, New York*

influenced by the decorative theory of the rugs of the Mamluks, whose example remains decisive as regards the color pitch as well. The character of the wool differs slightly, goat's hair is used for warp, weft and pile and, to begin with, the borders of these so-called "checkerboard rugs" diverge completely and are decidedly Anatolian in their outlook. They display small cartouches between stiff arabesques, palmettes or undulating vines

54. So-called "Checkerboard" Rug
Formerly in the Davanzati Palace, Florence

in a thoroughly un-Egyptian treatment. The guard stripes too are adapted rather to the Asia Minor scheme. Nevertheless, these weavings must not be considered simply as Anatolian imitations of the Cairene manner, for they have the same Senna knotting as the rugs from Egypt.

In a few Venetian paintings (e. g. by Lorenzo Lotto in the National Gallery, London, and by F. Torbido in the Vienna Academy) it must have been these rugs that were reproduced, rather than Mamluk designs; transitional stages from one to the other are represented by two originals in the Vienna Museum among others. Characteristic examples, which differ from each other merely in the number of their panels — from 3 to 35 — are not scarce; they may be found in Berlin (Islamic Department), Washington (Textile Museum), Florence (Bardini Museum) and in various public and private collections (Fig. 54). An interesting 17th century variation, doubtless from Asia Minor, is the property of the Islamic Museum in Cairo (Fig. 55).

55. Anatolian Version of the "Checkerboard" Rugs
Museum of Islamic Art, Cairo

It can easily be imagined that this class arose in a center which received its influences not only from Egypt but from Asia Minor as well; where this is to be sought for remains an enigma. The author considers it quite possible that it could have been this class that was meant by the term "tappeti rodioti", of which there is mention made in Venetian inventories of the 15th and 16th centuries, and that in the cross depicted in the centers of the repetitive star-motives we may recognize the emblem of the Order of St. John, which was resident in Rhodes until 1526. Even if this supposition should prove to be correct, it would naturally be understood merely that the rugs were made up primarily for the Knights Hospitalers of Rhodes, and not that they were manufactured somewhere on the island itself, so the question of their localization remains just as unsettled as before.

THE CARPETS OF PERSIA

Early Persian Rugs

A number of textiles were discovered a few years ago by Prof. Rudenko in a kurgan, or sepulchral mound, in the Altai district of Siberia, in inner chambers, frozen solid, together with other objects which might well have pertained to the burial of a Scythian king. Among these a rug some 6'6" × 6'3" in size caused a particular sensation. In few color tones, with red predominant, it contains in its field ornamented squares arranged checkerboard-fashion; around these a frieze of grazing stags or elk. The border displays a repeat of riders and men on foot with horses; the outer guard stripe, griffin medallions. According to the circumstances of this discovery the fabric was assumed to date from the 5th century B. C., and the somewhat primitive — Scythian? — variation on Assyrian-Achaemenid themes seemed to corroborate this. If, and on this score the most precise investigation still seems to be called for, as a matter of fact the pile of the rug was not obtained, perchance, through the shearing of loops but, as was published, by authentic and astonishingly fine knotting — in the so-called Ghiordes knot — then we are faced with what is by far the earliest production in this technique and must fundamentally revise our conceptions regarding the origins of the Oriental rug.

Hitherto we merely knew that in Persia in pre-Islamic times kilim-weaving and embroidery had achieved conspicuous heights; the famed "Springtime of Chosroes", which was suspended from the high vault of the palace of the Sassanians at Ctesiphon and which aroused the admiration of the conquering Arabs, assuredly was no knotted carpet. Too, we possess evidence of no sort that the art of knotting was indigenous in the Iranian area in the Early Middle Ages and we did have grounds for the assumption that the Seljuks, when they attained to sovereignty, brought the vogue for carpets along from their motherland in Turkestan in the 11th century for the first, and that from this time forward, through the stabilization of whole generations of weavers, this was by degrees evolved into a flourishing industry. Trustworthy accounts from literary sources which might confirm this reasoning are not yet at our disposal, and parallels with other art products offer us no more reliable support.

We cannot refer to representations of rugs in Persian miniature paintings until after the close of the 14th century, but in the course of the 15th century they become reasonably abundant. Of course it will be only with circumspection that we shall make use of their presence here as verification of the designs that were usual at that time; for doubtless in many cases the artists did not copy minutely

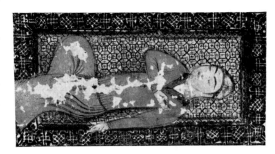

56. Detail from a Persian Miniature Painting (1420)   *State Museums, Berlin*

any actual floor-covering, but merely interpreted them in a rather free and easy manner or even invented them. Regardless of this, the regular repetition of certain definite ornamental forms by the most diverse book-illuminators permits us satisfactory conclusions regarding their actual decorative stock-in-trade. According to these reproductions the field

57. Detail from a Persian Miniature Painting (1429)   *Gulistan Museum, Teheran*

appears to have been filled either with a simple scale-pattern or latticework or else with a continuous and usually rather loose plaited design, in which stars, rosettes, hexagons or other incidental motives were interspersed (Figs. 56, 57). Now and then there is originated in this way one of those cross and star effects with multiple modifications that seem so akin to the Persian tile floors, or in other cases, again, we will be reminded of the octagon systems of Turkoman and Anatolian rugs.

The interlaced ribbon borders cannot deny their inception from the decorative remodelling of Cufic characters and display forms quite similar to those with which we have become acquainted among the so-called Holbein rugs. Yet unlike these, the Persian examples at this early date could already offer clear corner solutions by means of which was produced a self-enclosed frame for the field, a treatment which always remained unfamiliar to the weavers of Anatolia. From their reflections in the miniature paintings of the late 15th century we can clearly perceive just how these compositions of interwoven bands are gradually translated into arabesque and palmette forms. Then too there already appears in the field from time to time that medallion layout which constitutes the characteristic hallmark of Persian carpet production during their classical golden age under the Safavids in the 16th and 17th centuries.

Medallion Carpets

The Persian medallion carpet, a professional production of a very high order, is not in its conception any folk-art pursued by nomads or peasants, but doubtless took its origin from and was perfected in the closest relationship with other ornamental treatments. It presupposes a designer's skill and clear space-disposition and above all it permits its indebtedness to the art of book decoration to be plainly understood. Obvious is the correspondence with the title pages, ornamental leaves and chapter headings of the manuscripts of the 15th—16th centuries, just as it is also with the setting out of their bindings, and certainly in many cases the artists versed in these art forms must have themselves supplied preliminary sketches for the carpets. The only point still open to question is whether the introduction of the medallion scheme resulted from private operations or in the court manufactories. The latter is the more plausible, for in the workshops which were connected with the seats of the court (Herat, Tabriz, Kazvin, Ispahan etc.) the book-artists enjoyed great prestige and therefore could most easily take over the task of influencing whatever might be taking form upon the weaving and knotting looms.

The medallion style enjoined a rupture with the rule that had been quite universally observed up to that time: that the field of a rug be handled as if it were a piece cut from a continuous patterning, be this with geometric or with floral motives. In Anatolia this concept always remained authoritative, even with the introduction of medallion or star forms as in the Ushaks (see above). In Persia, on the other hand, the surface of the carpet now was planned in such a way that the decorative scheme was deployed symmetrically in all four directions from one dominant central motive, whereby the fashioning of the centerpiece allowed the most varied possibilities. The carpet thus arranged formed an ideal covering for the floor, inasmuch as it produced the same effect, when placed in a room which was dimensioned to it on all four sides, through concentrating one's glance, which was not the case — and mark well that this was quite intentional — in progressive or repetitive designs. Obligatory therewith became a stronger accentuation of the border to ensure contrast with the field in both color and drawing and enclose it as a frame does a painting.

The localization of the existent medallion carpets has more than once been attempted, but up to now it has still met with no convincing success. This study is less dependent upon peculiarities in the designing — e. g. whether with or without animal decoration — than on the materials employed, the chromatic range, the austerity or fluidity of the drawing and other technical factors. At the present time the general inclination is to trace back one reasonably uniform group with severe linear treatment and a related palette to Tabriz, and the majority of those knotted in silk, on the other hand, to Kashan. However, whether a further group with softer wool and a warmer color-key was actually native to Herat still remains just as unsettled as the question of the attribution of certain other families of carpets to Kirman. Fewer difficulties arise as to the dating. Through their occurrence in miniature paintings since the late 15th century and through accurate statements of the year of the weaving on at least two of the most important pieces we find ourselves rather reliably oriented. The golden age of the class doubtless falls within the first half of the 16th century.

It can certainly be assumed that originally the medallion carpets displayed a decorative scheme that was exclusively floral. Pieces so designed are marked by clever layout of the surface, by clean draftsmanship and tasteful formalization of the leaf and blossom motif borne upon delicate vines, as well as by discreetly weighed color contrasts. The dominant central shield, which often takes up the entire breadth of the field, assumes diverse shapes: as a many-pointed star or as an oval or round with rippled contour, and is detailed in a multitude of ways, always with an inner motif

58. Medallion Carpet with Vine Scrolling   *Textile Museum, Washington*

59. Medallion Carpet with Floral Decoration   *Musée des Arts Décoratifs, Paris*

of contrasting color. It is difficult to decide whether the large medallion came originally upon the scene complete in itself or whether it appeared from the very start with those characteristic pendants which jut out into the field towards both ends of the carpet, and which unmistakably were inspired by the art of the bookbinder. Frequently corner-pieces are also added to the design, which, however, usually do not represent true segments from the central figure.

A distinct group of this character which, despite the ever-varied modelling of its medallions, shows a tight interrelationship in its accentuation of spiral vines, in its favoring of arabesque forms and in other individual peculiarities, is drawn even more closely together through a very similar border treatment. In extraordinarily stiff drawing, reciprocally placed palmettes rest upon trailing stems which tend towards the arabesque, in a vivid color effect; in every instance the two guard stripes are, in fact, of different designs. The examples which constitute this group (in the Islamic Collection in Berlin, in the Victoria and Albert Museum in London, and in various American collections; see Fig. 58) must have originated during the first third of the 16th century in Northwest Persia, perhaps in Tabriz itself. To these is allied a second type which uses cloud bands in the field, and in the borders little medallions and rosettes connected by a sort of an astragal or included in cartouche combinations, frequently even in a doubled arrangement. A very fine specimen of this kind is in the Museum of Decorative Arts in Paris (Fig. 59); others are owned by Prince Yusuf Kemal in Cairo and by J. V. McMullan (now in the Art Institute, Chicago), for example.

A unique place among these rugs is occupied by the state carpet, 26'6" × 13'7" in size, which came to the Metropolitan Museum from the ducal house of Anhalt (Fig. 60). The gleaming, golden-yellow ground is effectively set off by the red of the border and the similarly red, scalloped, circular medallion, while one section of the pendants and the inner guard stripe are done in a clear blue. The arabesque is predominant in the decorative scheme of this carpet, and in the border it appears in a marvelously light and elegant arrangement; in the field it is given greater emphasis and interpolated with cloud bands and with birds which have been scattered here and there quite imperceptibly. There can be no question but that here we are dealing with the product of a court loom of the first half of the 16th century and if this, as has been assumed, was

60. Medallion Carpet with Arabesques   *Metropolitan Museum, New York*

61. The Ardebil Carpet (1539)   *Victoria and Albert Museum, London*

62. Medallion Rug in Silk   *Metropolitan Museum, New York*

located at Tabriz, the carpets mentioned previously must have been woven in a different establishment, though in the same neighborhood.

Still more imposing, 36'6" long, and matchless in its execution is the famed carpet which was made at Shah Tahmasp's direction for the sepulchral mosque of Sheikh Safi in Ardebil and which bears, besides the date A. H. 946 (1539 A. D.), the name of the artist as well, Maksud of Kashan. This carpet is now in the Victoria and Albert Museum in London (Fig. 61). Upon its dark blue field, which is entirely covered by a dense vine-scrolling with stylized peonies and lotus blossoms, lies a sixteen-pointed star ornamented with arabesques and cloud bands on a yellow ground; to the projecting points of this star is affixed a garland of pointed ovals, of varied interior design and coloring, while along the longitudinal axis there hangs down also towards either end of the carpet a vase-shaped mosque lamp. Segments of the central motif are repeated in the corners. The border has a colorful alternation of cartouches with cloud bands and octofoils with arabesques upon a dark ground. The inner guard stripe shows cloud bands placed reciprocally; the outer, palmette-flowers on large arabesques, whose delineation is very similar, but much more buoyant and graceful than in the borders of the group reviewed above. That the master, a native of Kashan, did not carry out this sublime triumph of the art of knotting in his home city but in Tabriz, is today scarcely still open to question. A companion piece of identical composition, but severely reduced and mutilated, turned up in America several decades ago and is now in the Los Angeles County Museum, the gift of J. Paul Getty of Santa Monica, California.

Kashan has entered its claim to a series of medallion rugs, usually of smaller dimensions (about 8' × 4'6"), which are woven entirely in silk. The centerpiece usually has a four-lobed outline, with but a scarcely noticeable intimation of the pendants which otherwise are so customary, yet occasionally at a short distance away from it there will be a conspicuous enclosing ribbon-scroll set with large blossoms (e. g. in the Bavarian National Museum and in the Metropolitan Museum, Fig. 62), that takes up almost the whole of the field, which is also provided with corner segments. An example in the Museum of the Gobelins in Paris amid the vine-scrolling of its ground, aside from the customary flowers and foliage, shows with especial clarity the clenched form of that symbol adopted from China, the "tchi", which is more familiar to us in its Iranian formalization as the cloud

band. The borders bring into currency large and small palmette-flowers
upon a background sprinkled with ornament.

Medallion carpets, as we have learned to know them in this short
sketch, can be authenticated with the most trifling variations in Persian
miniature paintings of the first half of the 16th century: as from the hand
of the artist Shaikh-zada in a Hafiz edition of 1510—1520, in a manuscript
dated 1522 in the National
Museum at Teheran, from a page
in the Metropolitan Museum
(Fig. 63) deriving from about
1525, in a manuscript of the
year 1533 and in other places.
That this type had already been
developed by about the end of
the 15th century follows from
the fact that at that time designs
which were essentially more
complex were already being
reproduced (see under compartment carpets).

63. Detail from a Persian Miniature Painting
Metropolitan Museum, New York

Differing somewhat from the others, but probably produced likewise in
Kashan, is a woolen rug on silk warp in the possession of Baron Albert
Rothschild in Vienna, whose central star reveals an additional inner disk
with pheasants among scattered blossoms; the border consists of oblong
cartouches and lobed rosettes, and in the inner guard stripe appear Persian
verses (3rd edit., Fig. 29). Again, an example in the Museum of Decorative
Arts in Paris shows four peacocks in a cruciform arrangement within the
central medallion and Persian texts placed more conspicuously in the
panels of the border itself (3rd edit., Fig. 10). A further example of the
introduction into the classic Kashan design of an animated decor presents
itself in the splendid silk rug which has found its way into the Gulbenkian
Collection from the Berlin Museum of Decorative Arts. This piece displays
in its field dramatic, rousing animal combats; dragon and phoenix in the
central quatrefoil; in the deep-green border, instead of undulating ribbons,
spiritedly drawn pheasants confront the great floral palmettes (Fig. 64).

In the same way as in the silk rugs, the transition from the purely floral
to a decorative scheme interpolated with animal figures can be established

also among those knotted in wool, and this precedent too was certainly established during the first half of the 16th century. In a few examples, which achieve a remarkably sumptuous appearance through being

64. Medallion Rug in Silk   *Gulbenkian Collection, London*

brocaded with silver threads, their relationship with the trend that emanated from Kashan becomes quite evident in the form of their medallions, the mode of enlivenment of their fields, and above all in the employment of cartouches with Persian verses in their borders. As salient masterpieces we will mention here rugs in the possession of Baron Rothschild in Paris (Fig. 65), in the Metropolitan Museum (Fig. 66) and — probably of a somewhat later date — in the Musée des Tissus in Lyons (Fig. 67). We will find the cartouches with verses in a woolen rug at the Hermitage (from the Lobanow Collection, 3rd edit., Figs. 6/7) to be

65. Medallion Rug with Animals and Inscribed Verses   *Baron Rothschild, Paris*

consummate in their calligraphy and singularly impressive. The arabesque medallion of this piece is still closely related to the purely ornamental Kashan productions, whereas amid the vine-scrolling of the field dragons, leopards, harts and jackals wheel about and in the corners pheasants, parrots and cranes attacked by falcons are stirring.

All sorts of beasts are scattered in an entirely different fashion over the red field of a carpet with the stiffly drawn arabesque border so characteristic of Northwest Persia (Survey, Pl. 1148), while arabesques and cloud bands fill the yellow central medallion. From the same neighborhood arose two beautiful pieces of the early 16th century with white grounds that are almost coincident in design. Of this pair one, formerly in the Berlin Museum, burned during the war and the other belongs to Count Bucquoi in Vienna (Fig. 68). Its field displays among floral vines single animals well-

66. Medallion Carpet with Animals and Inscribed Verses
Metropolitan Museum, New York

studied from nature and battling Far Eastern kylins; the great bright red, eight-pointed star with its concentric inner repeat and its double pendants at either end are filled with arabesques and blossomwork. In the border the exuberant floral scheme is loosely organized in the favorite system of cartouches and lobed octagons.

The application of animal decoration, which we will understand was a matter of course only in carpets that were destined for profane use, and not in those for religious places, soon led to the thought of embellishing the field with trees and shrubbery which would form the background provided for the animals, instead of the floral vines used hitherto. This emphasis upon the idea of a garden is carried into effect in a remarkably impressive manner in a few stately specimens which we count among the most outstanding achievements of the knotter's art, and which presumably all originated together in the Tabriz district shortly before 1550. In the first of these, which is owned by Prince Schwarzenberg in Vienna (Fig. 69), in a dense tangle of cypresses, plane-

67. Medallion Rug with Inscribed Verses
Musée des Tissus, Lyons

trees, fruit trees and coverts are interspersed lions, leopards, phoenixes and smaller birds, while in the almost square central shield ducks appear in pairs, enveloped by an arabesque creeper, and in the oblong pendants, confronted peacocks. The border displays in a sort of a reciprocal crown design an alternation of red and white surfaces adorned with birds among blossoms, cloud bands and animal-masks in the form of palmettes. Of wholly similar plan in field and border, with a richer trove of animals, but without the ducks in the centerpiece, was a carpet with a green ground, a large fragment of which hangs in the Philadelphia Museum (Williams Collection). To the same school, moreover, belonged a magnificent example,

one half of which is in the Cathedral at Cracow, the other in the Paris
Museum of Decorative Arts. This has a field of yellow, a red medallion, and
a very freely composed red border, which is enlivened with birds and
quadrupeds amid flowering shrubs and palmettes (Fig. 70).

68. Medallion Carpet with Animals (destroyed)   *Formerly State Museums, Berlin*

A step more advanced in decorative scheme, but bearing the closest
time and place relationship to the group just under discussion, come a pair
of carpets, of which one specimen in perfect preservation has passed on
from the Mackay Collection to Los Angeles. The other, somewhat reduced,
which had been acquired for the Berlin Museum by W. v. Bode from a
synagogue in Genoa, was so shattered during the Second World War that

from its remnants scarcely a quarter of the original surface could be reconstructed (Fig. 71). The fauna, active here among trees of various kinds upon a ground of white, is particularly diverse: the lion, the panther, the

69. Medallion Carpet with Animals   *Prince Schwarzenberg, Vienna*

bull, the stag, the ibex, the jackal, the hare and the dog show excellent observation on the part of the designer. Beside these appear the dragon, phoenix, stag- and lion-kylins, and on the boughs apes and birds. The only basic innovation consists in filling up the large medallion with cranes which stride along, fly away, or merely flutter about, while in their midst

101

fawns bed down among cloud bands and cloud-knots; and then too in the portrayal of two genii in human form in each of the four corner elements (varied somewhat from one end of the rug to the other). In the dark-blue

70. Medallion Carpet with Animals   *Musée des Arts Décoratifs, Paris*

border floral vines and palmettes are discreetly marshalled by shapely arabesques. A somewhat later mutation of this same concept, with greater accentuation of the towering cypresses and with repeats of the struggle

102

71. Medallion Carpet with Animals *County Museum, Los Angeles*

72. Medallion Carpet with Animals and Genii   *Poldi Pezzoli Museum, Milan*

between dragon and phoenix in the central star as well as in the border, is presented by the great carpet from Mantes Cathedral now in the Louvre.

By contrast, the unquestionably earlier carpet in the Poldi Pezzoli Museum in Milan, aside from the many features which correspond, shows

73. Medallion Rug with Animals and Genii   *Musée des Tissus, Lyons*

such frequent deviations from the current scheme that it can scarcely have originated in Northwest Persia (Fig. 72). The medallion, here of somewhat reduced proportions, decorated with flowers and birds, has no pendants, but at some distance away from it we espy pairs of genii crouching beside a vase with a fan-like superstructure and a fantastic canopy above it, of a symbolic significance that would be difficult to explain. The balance of the field is filled with ramose flowering trees, together with dragons, tigers and

105

74. Medallion Carpet with Animals   *State Museums, Berlin*

lions amid blossomwork; we miss the cypresses which have been so customary in the other rugs. The border offers us large palmettes on sweeping arabesques within which are animal figures; the inner guard, a continuous Persian text. The material is the finest of wool in such dense knotting that in the first edition of this handbook it was designated erroneously as silk. The same is true of a rug in Lyons, brocaded with gold and silver thread, which, in addition to a border of almost identical design, likewise exhibits genie-forms; here, to be sure, these occur in the center-piece, and in the field are animals both singly and in combat (Fig. 73).

Towards the end of the 16th century the theme of the medallion carpet with animals received further modification in yet another production center (Kazvin?), this time without the usual enrichment of the store of forms, yet dependent in composition upon the earlier school, and evidently again with novel ideas and more perfect technical execution. To this type belong examples in the Hermitage, in the Victoria and Albert Museum (with three genii in each corner), in the Berlin Museum (formerly in the Cassirer Collection, with palmettes formed by pairs of peacocks and of fishes in the border, Fig. 74), in the Osma Collection (Madrid), in that of the Countess of Béhague etc. Prince Sanguszko's carpet, now on loan to the Metropolitan Museum richer in coloring than those just mentioned, is nevertheless related to them. It has pairs of genii in small medallions in centerpiece and border and pairs of riders a hunting in each of its four corners (Survey, Pl. 1206, dating quite certainly from about 1600). The latter motif brings us in turn to the category of the figure or hunting carpets in which, as we shall presently see, this theme had already been handled in the "grand style" half a century before.

When, in addition to the figures of animals, human forms also were first admitted within the compass of the knotting art, or even thought desirable for such a purpose, there was presented to the artisans thereby a new opportunity for displaying their skill, even though in this case still more firmly than before they were to find themselves referred to the assistance of the book-illuminator. In fact the weavers received some inspiration from time to time from those miniaturists who were furnishing sketches for the court manufactory in Tabriz, and indeed Shah Tahmasp, who was an able draftsman, may well have taken a hand himself in this respect. In Tabriz, his capital, at all events, must have originated the great hunting carpet which first came to notice about 1925 and is now exhibited in the Poldi

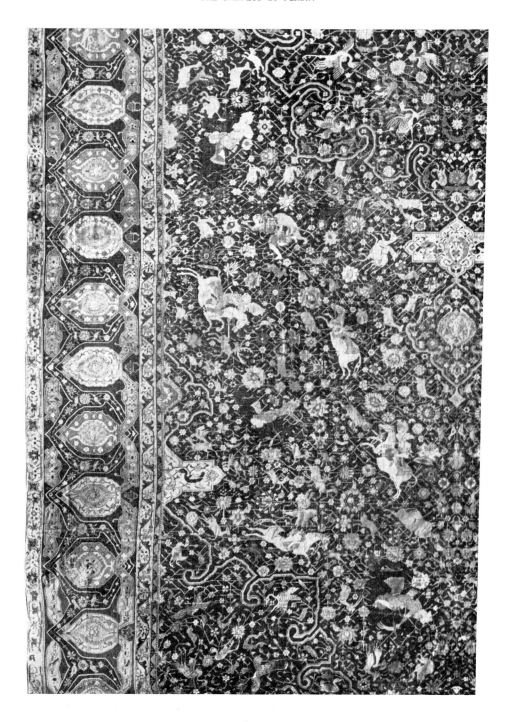

75. Medallion Carpet with Hunting Scenes (1542)   *Poldi Pezzoli Museum, Milan*

76. Field Decor of a Silken Medallion Carpet with Hunting Scenes
Austrian Museum of Applied Arts, Vienna

Pezzoli Museum (Fig. 75). Upon a dark-blue field in bold colors, interspersed with delicate floral vines, all sorts of game are represented, which in turn are hunted with bow or lance by horsemen of the most varied deportment, or sometimes too are harried by falcons; beaters who are assailed by panthers appear also. The red, sharply incised centerpiece, in much the same way as in the Mackay carpet, is filled with flying cranes, ducks and cloud bands, and has two-part pendants. A true segment of this centerpiece and of the pendants as well is repeated in each corner and through this, just as through the bisection of the palmettes wherever they meet the border, there is indicated a continuity of design which otherwise is not customary among Persian medallion carpets, but which, on the other hand, is characteristic of the Ushaks, for instance. In the precise center of the surface is reserved a little cartouche which bears the signature of the fabricator, Ghiyâth-ed-dîn Djâmi, and dating in a year which can be read either as A. H. 929 (1523 A. D.) or as A. H. 949 (1542/43 A. D.). On stylistic grounds one might give the preference to the later date, to which is better suited, primarily, this border of stiff arabesques and palmettes in astonishingly austere and commonplace drawing, and the utterly inadequate treatment of its corners. This will allow at least a few years' advantage to the Ardebil carpet, so incomparable in quality (see above).

Wholly knotted in silk and brocaded in part with gilded silver threads is our next subject, the most celebrated of all figure carpets, and in many ways it has been generally regarded as the most outstanding achievement of this field of art (Figs. 76, 77). Once court-property of the Hapsburgs, it is now in the Museum of Applied Arts in Vienna. Here the salmon-colored ground is, just as in the Milan example, filled with riders in pursuit of all manner of game, but whereas there the strictest symmetry prevails in the treatment of the figures both as to drawing and as to color, here they are disposed more freely about the surface and symmetry extends only to their repetition from the center as towards the two ends of the carpet, with counterchange of color. In the green centerpiece, echoed exactly in the corner quadrants, pairs of dragons and phoenixes gape at one another, while in the border two seated genii, serving each other, repeat regularly upon a background of luxurious ornament. Even if we disregard the classical perfection of its execution, it becomes quite clear that this carpet has originated in some court manufactory — perhaps at Kashan — at just about the middle of the 16th century, because of the "stick" turbans of the horsemen, which in later years will no longer be the fashion. More difficult to resolve is the question of whether the cartoon for this rug can be attributed to Sultan Muhammad or to some other of the artists at the court of Shah Tahmasp.

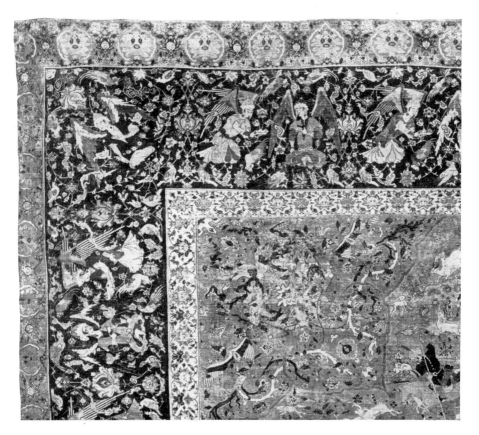

77. Genie Border of the Silken Medallion Carpet with Hunting Scenes
Austrian Museum of Applied Arts, Vienna

A second silken, silver-interwoven hunting carpet, obviously of like origin, passed from the ownership of the Marchese Torrigiani, who sold it for a ridiculous price, about 1879, via the antiquary Bardini, to Baron Adolphe Rothschild in Paris, still at a preposterously low figure. The green field of this carpet displays mounted hunters again, but this time fewer in number than at Vienna. The salmon-colored medallion, which recurs segmentally in the corners, presents individualistic leopard-dragons in conflict with the simurg (phoenix); the red border, human figures with "stick" turbans in four different attitudes (Sarre-Trenkwald II, Pl. 24—26). No

111

horsemen this time, but men grappling with lions amid many cloud bands and a few game animals occupy the red field of still another silk carpet in the Castle at Stockholm, whose olive-green border contains animals within spiral vines between almond-trees, whereas the white central star, repeated

78. So-called Portuguese Carpet (destroyed)   *Formerly State Museums, Berlin*

in the corners, is enlivened with a free arabesque-work. We will assign this state carpet to the same looms as both of the preceding, but fix it somewhat later in time.

That other solutions, even more diverse, for this figure carpet theme were discovered in Persia towards the middle of the 16th century, is evident

112

Persian Arabesque Carpet   *State Museums, Berlin*

from a fragment which belonged to Baron Hatvany in Budapest (Survey Pl. 1141). The white ground with cypresses and other trees, among which animals appear either singly or in combat with one another, is quite familiar to us here from one of the groups which we have cited. The surprise in this case exists in the unique appropriation of the blue centerpiece by a scene which is completely graphic in its composition and is enacted in a garden pavilion. Unfortunately, this scene can no longer be reconstructed, but without a doubt the eleven persons represented with "stick" turbans, each of whom has been characterized in a different manner, form part of a court reception, whose focus was provided by the enthroned prince. In a marginal cartouche we recognize among cloud bands a simurg, which holds an antelope in its grasp. The material is wool. Tabriz is accepted, quite properly, as the place of its origin; the cartoon was certainly from one of the court painters who were established there.

In the 17th century the medallion scheme, in so far as it was generally still retained, found itself unmistakably on the downgrade. Among the vegetal designs the arabesque yields more and more to an uncertainly handled blossomwork. In animal carpets the decor often is out of balance; at times overloaded, in other cases invention-poor, but above all else the borders, which frequently are much subdivided, cause us to feel the lack of the strict discipline of the classic golden age. The so-called *Portuguese* carpets, which probably were produced in Southern Persia, compose a separate group at this time. In these — always with an elongated format — the centerpiece is expanded longitudinally to such an extent through concentric repeats in changing color that it scarcely spares room for the corner-sections, in which sailing vessels manned by Europeans are displayed. This motif has been connected by some students with an episode that was occasioned by the arrival of a Portuguese diplomatic mission in the Persian Gulf, and along with this they would have it that such rugs were intended for the Portuguese in Goa. That these pieces were actually made up in that enclave itself, and consequently upon Indian soil, as A. U. Pope assumes, is wholly improbable in view of their fashioning, which is purely Persian, with bold coloration. Of the less widely known examples of this class, the Berlin specimen has alas been completely destroyed (Fig. 78); similar carpets are in the Vienna Museum, the Musée des Tissus in Lyons, in the H. F. du Pont Winterthur Museum, near Wilmington, Del., and in English ownership (see Survey Pl. 1216). A piece of simpler design in the

Metropolitan Museum, perhaps a Caucasian copy, has animal figures in the spandrels (Fig. 79).

In addition to those rugs in which the centerpiece dominates the entire surface, others of early date have no doubt existed in which, by a repetition

79. Caucasian Version of the "Portuguese Carpets"
Metropolitan Museum, New York

of the medallion motif in accordance with a variety of formulas, more of a continuous patterning was created. We will set these aside for the moment and will take them up again in connection with the so-called compartment rugs (see below, p. 124).

Vine Scroll Patterns

We consider it appropriate to mention in conjunction with the medallion carpets two groups of knotted rugs of the classical era of the 16th and 17th centuries which are likewise strictly centralized in plan, notwithstanding

80. Arabesque Carpet (fragment)   *State Museums, Berlin*

that this is merely about a focal point which may be either imaginary or else but faintly indicated, and which under certain conditions may appear as a greatly reduced medallion. In this category, just a small one if we

81. Arabesque Carpet with Animals   *Formerly Bardini Collection, Florence*

number its examples, of *arabesque* rugs, the surface is taken over by buoyantly conducted, forked leafy vines, behind which the other ornamental shapes all recede into the background. A remarkably handsome and early fragment of this sort, interpolated with majestic cloud bands, once belonged to the Berlin Museum (destroyed in the war; Sarre-

116

Trenkwald II, Pl. 9). There has been preserved in the same collection a later example of small dimensions (Pl. IV) with spiral arabesque stems which group themselves symmetrically about a small central star. The border is

82. "Herat" Carpet with Metal Threads   *A. Cassirer Estate, Berlin*

of cartouches and quatrefoil rosettes, so familiar to us here from many a medallion carpet of the Tabriz School, to which this particular piece can be assigned without hesitation. Yet a third variety, again incomplete, does Berlin have to offer us, with fibrous arabesques in wire-like spirals which converge toward the center diamond-fashion, and with a border whose grandiose sweep suggests an imaginative interpretation of the so-called reciprocal *fleur-de-lis* or wall-cresting pattern (Fig. 80).

In one composition of this sort, in which two arabesque systems eventually interpenetrate one another, we will find animal figures interspersed through the design, as well as the usual flowers (Fig. 81). The class persisted on into the 19th century and evidently was a favorite in various centers. As regards the derivation of its ornament we can confirm several points of correspondence with book-illumination, as well as with the faïence mosaics which in the 16th and 17th centuries played an important

83. Detail from a Painting by F. Bol (1649)
Rijksmuseum, Amsterdam

role in architectural decoration in Northwest as well as in Central and Eastern Persia (Tabriz, Ardebil, Ispahan, Meshhed, Herat).

With respect to color arrangement, one or another of the arabesque designs is doubtless affiliated with the class of the so-called *Herat* rugs. As to these weavings, it still remains unproven whether they actually did originate in the capital of Khorassan, accredited as a carpet center, which had great significance under the Timurids as a cultural focus until about 1500, but then lost its political importance in favor of Tabriz. In the trade rugs of this class are known, probably quite unjustly, as "Ispahan rugs". Their characteristic hallmark is the tonal contrast created by a field that is almost universally red and a border of either dark-blue or dark-green. In lieu of the arabesques, which have well-nigh completely disappeared, here there are flowers borne upon thin spirals (peonies, the lotus, palmettes) which, interlaced with cloud bands, supply the decorative scheme. This deploys in all four directions from a central point which often is merely hinted at. Several notably sumptuous pieces are embroidered with metal thread (Fig. 82), others enlivened with animal motives. The material is always wool of warm and saturated coloring; the warp and weft are occasionally of silk. The borders are fashioned with great diversity and offer the easiest means of grouping

84. "Herat" Carpet with Animals   *Austrian Museum of Applied Arts, Vienna*

these rugs chronologically, a procedure which is also facilitated by their appearance in European paintings.

Whereas "Herat rugs" are very difficult to find among Italian artists, we meet with them from time to time among the Spanish masters (Velásquez, Coello, Moya), and then particularly in Rubens (Marie de

85. "Herat" Carpet with Animals   *Metropolitan Museum, New York*

Medici Cycle in the Louvre) and van Dyck (the children of Charles I at Windsor and in Dresden), who doubtless possessed such pieces of their own. They occur most frequently among Hollands genre painters of the 17th century, among whom we may mention here Vermeer, Terborch, Metsu, J. Steen, P. de Hooch, Codde, Netscher, Slingelant, Ochtervelt, E. v. d. Neer and Mieris. In a painting by F. Bol we note above one such "Herat rug", employed as a table-cover, the artist's signature and the date 1649 (Fig. 83). Original pieces have come to light in very great numbers, especially in Portugal and in Holland; these two countries had the closest commercial connections with Persia, and Armenian tradespeople, among whose imported wares Persian rugs were expressly mentioned, had established themselves in Lisbon and in Amsterdam.

As the noblest achievements of this type of weaving we must speak of an originally matched pair of rugs, of which one is in the Austrian Museum, the other, formerly in the possession of Mrs. Rockefeller McCormick, now in the Metropolitan Museum (Fig. 84). Among the floral palmettes of the field, which are incomparably diverse in size and form, and with which at times the cloud bands form novel combinations, we become aware of single animals and animals in combat. Facile vinework, conducted with a sure hand, fills the deep-green border; Persian verses adorn the inner guard. A fragment closely allied to this was formerly in the hands of D. Kelekian; this and a further scrap, which again is preserved in the Vienna Museum, and has a vigorous bordering of great palmettes and arabesque bands, obviously belong together. Similar additional fragments are in the Victoria and Albert Museum and in the museum at Reichenberg. Animal motives are exceptionally dominant in a rug from the Sarre Collection, which was obtained from Ardebil and whose exact counterpart is in the Metropolitan Museum, with a repeat design that has no proper center and a very graceful cloud band border (Fig. 85).

All of the specimens cited must have been manufactured by about the middle of the 16th century, and were followed by those with purely floral decoration. These display less variety in their fields than in their borders. Some still retain the system, familiar here from other classes, of alternating cartouches with rosette-medallions, and sometimes this appears in a multiple arrangement. Others favor the bold accent, popular also in Northwest Persia, of large palmettes between spirited arabesques which at times are heavy, at others, graceful; we can follow the course of development by which these gradually were transformed into simple lancet leaves (see Fig. 87). These same feathery, sweeping fronds become ever more important in the field-decor as well; whereas in the beginning they still appear beside the cloud bands quite discreetly (Fig. 86), during the 17th century they crowd these out entirely (Fig. 87) and become ever more conspicuous in the design (Fig. 88).

Most abundant are the borders which are decidedly floral, with palmette-forms of various sizes. In the earlier examples these still rest upon finely-managed, delicate vines, now and then with little birds

86. So-called Herat Rug   *Formerly Dr. Alsberg, Berlin*

scattered amongst them; in the course of the 17th century the cohesion is
gradually relaxed so that finally the figures stand quite stiff and detached
in their frame about a field which, of course, also by now bears every
indication of torpidity.

Hundreds of specimens of this class still survive, some of great size
indeed, often a whole series of them in one place — for example, about

122

40 pieces in the museum at Lisbon, more than a dozen at Coimbra, and in the Corcoran Gallery in Washington — and despite their many variations, their provenance from one and the same production center is made quite

87. So-called Herat Carpet

certain through the uniformity of their materials and especially through the color harmonies which they share. It is supposed by most scholars today that the actual place where this center should be sought is in Herat, and the fact that products of the 19th century which bear this place-name in the trade still permit their distant descent from old examples of this school to be divined — especially in the so-called "Herati" borders — seems to bear witness for this assumption. By way of exception, in the classic era there

123

appear at times coloristic variants — as, for instance, in a rug with blue
ground and red border, which is in the Islamic Museum in Cairo — and then
too, typical Herat design has been taken up from time to time by other
centers.

88. So-called Herat Rug

Compartment Designs

The distinctive character of the celebrated Ardebil carpet, which dates
from the year 1539, consists in the encirclement of its great central star by
a crown of small, pointed-oval medallions, which are repeated in the corner
segments. In an animal carpet belonging to the Victoria and Albert Museum,
which survives only in a fragmentary state, a like decorative thought
seems to have led to the independence of these oval panels which had
originally been thought of as mere satellites. As a matter of fact, however,
such elements already appear in the early 16th century, and certainly with

124

89. Carpet with Several Medallions   *Victoria and Albert Museum, London*

a mediative function, in a carpet with several medallions in the same museum, which must be ranked among the most brilliant performances of the art of knotting in Persia (Fig. 89).

In this instance the field exhibits along its longitudinal axis, in a quite unique way, two star medallions of moderate size filled with arabesque trails, and portions of these are repeated in the corners and along the side-margins. Oval medallions, each with a pair of birds on flowery branches, establish a connection between these stars, but in such a way that room has been left in the center of the field for a small circular pool with fishes. To this pool is affixed, both above and below, a vase of flowers which is combined with lions and dragons in a most peculiar manner and contains a pair of peacocks. This motif repeats down to the smallest details, at least in part, so that the whole effect produced is that of a composition which is not centralized but continuous. The border, which employs a grandly sweeping, reciprocal treatment, filled with animals and cloud bands, is extraordinarily close to that of the Schwarzenberg carpet (Fig. 69), and it is to be assumed that the two pieces originated in the same neighborhood, the London carpet most probably in the court manufactory at Tabriz. An incompletely preserved example in the Bardini Museum in Florence, with dragon and phoenix in the oval panels and medallions of various other forms upon a ground adorned with trees and enlivened by animals, this time with inscribed cartouches in the border, belongs unmistakably to the same school.

Perhaps we will not go far astray if we consider the state carpet just described as the forerunner of the true compartment carpets. In these the entire field is furnished with diminutive medallions, diverse in their contour and arrangement, in such fashion that it may be clearly recognized as merely a portion of a design that could have been continued indefinitely. Only a few examples of this kind have come down to us, the most interesting being that in the Metropolitan Museum (Fig. 90; a poorly preserved companion piece is in the Textile Museum in Lyons). Lobed octagons with the dragon and phoenix serve as centers for the repeated, starlike compartment groupings; other small panels display lions or cranes amid vine scrolls which, in most delicate handling, also animate the white ground visible between the compartments. The dragon motif again fills the lobed rosettes of the border, while in the adjoining cartouches the cloud band holds sway. The method by which the corner solutions are worked out in this case — through a panel that turns the corner — draws our attention with especial clarity to the drafts that have been made upon the art of bookbinding; the planning of the field with cartouches which are isolated and do not quite come into contact with one another does also forcibly bring to mind the bookbinder's stamping technique and his dies of various outlines. Cartouches similarly grouped, with floral ornament

90. "Compartment Carpet"   *Metropolitan Museum, New York*

exclusively, are displayed in a carpet with a prominent star-shaped center-piece and arabesque border, dating from the 16th century (it used to belong to Beghian, Survey Pl. 1125).

That carpets with more than one medallion had already made their appearance in Persia before the end of the 15th century is indicated by the representation of such a piece in a miniature by the renowned Bihzad, dated 1488 (Fig. 91). This shows three quatrefoils of equal size and filled with ornamentation, side by side, with decoration on a smaller scale between these, and a plaited-ribbon border, as seems to have generally been the custom in the 15th century. The painter may have redrafted various details quite arbitrarily, or on the other hand, as this very Bihzad always endeavors to portray everything just as true to life as he possibly can, it would seem quite reasonable that in this case he has freely invented the rug design submitted here.

91. Detail from a Miniature Painting by Bihzâd (1488)
Egyptian Library, Cairo

Compartment composition is carried out in a different way in Countess Clam-Gallas's carpet in Vienna, so very charming in its coloring (now in the Museum of Applied Arts there, Fig. 92): rows of quatrefoils, filled with palmette-blossoms or cloud bands, alternate with rows of curved plaquettes, in which confronted peacocks or pheasants are in turn alternated with arabesque emblems, while little pomegranate and almond-trees enliven the spaces between. The border again has the customary arrangement of oblong cartouches and rosettes. A compartment carpet whose panels are tightly consolidated, exceptionally varied in their coloring, adorned principally with palmette-flowers and arranged in cruciform repeats, coming rather closer to the vase carpets (see below) than to the medallion group, has come to the Metropolitan Museum from the Havemeyer Collection (Fig. 93, in color: Survey Pl. 1223). Akin to this is a specimen with a fluid sort of patterning, which is uniformly continuous over the entire field, in the Deering Collection (Survey Pl. 1239).

128

92. "Compartment Carpet"   *Austrian Museum of Applied Arts, Vienna*

What is more, there is a unique woolen carpet in the possession of the Duke of Buccleuch (Fig. 94) which should be ranked with the group with which we are now dealing. In small oval medallions mounted falconers, musicians or pairs of revelers are repeated; in conjoined shields, birds standing or else flying over a ground-filling of lions, leopards, ibexes and foxes amid varied branches of trees. The motives which mirror one another

93. "Compartment Carpet"   *Metropolitan Museum, New York*

accross the center line of the carpet have been made to correspond in reverse, an ordinary treatment among textiles, and the entire arrangement is not centralized, but continuous. The rosettes in the border are made up of interlaced dragons, while dragon and phoenix face each other in the cartouches. This carpet is very closely related to that medallion group which tentatively has been traced back to Kazvin and surely must date from the very end of the 16th century. A rug in the Textile Museum in Lyons is very similar in the composition of its field, but its border is quite divergent (with genie-medallions among arabesque trails).

130

94. "Compartment Carpet" with Figures   *The Duke of Buccleuch, England*

Rugs with Progressive Designs

Besides those carpets which have a centered composition, and this has been the rule with such classes as we have dealt with up to this point, pieces whose patterning was progressive were also normal in Persia at

95. So-called Vase Carpet　　　　　　　　　　　　*Museum of Islamic Art, Istanbul*

quite an early date. These gave currency to a vocabulary of forms which were almost exclusively floral, and these forms of course were of peculiar opulence. The most important group consists of the so-called *vase* carpets,

96. So-called Vase Carpet (destroyed) *Formerly State Museums, Berlin*

which are counted as among the most attractive products of the classic Iranian art of knotting. The field layout which is characteristic of their first phase is a diamond network formed by lanceolate leaves, much like

133

that which we found among the so-called dragon carpets (see above, p. 60). Upon a ground of counterchanged coloring, each of the diamond-shaped lozenges contains four diversely-fashioned motives which are joined together by short stems. Aside from palmettes and rosettes in numerous variations, stylized lilies appear and at intervals small vases with flowers in them, which have provided a name for the entire class. This system is carried out with particular clarity in an example which has been preserved in the Istanbul Museum (Fig. 95).

The next step beyond this is represented by two rugs of identical design, of which one, formerly in the Berlin Schloßmuseum, unfortunately was destroyed by fire in 1945 (Fig. 96); the other, which is incomplete, is to be found in Glasgow (in the possession of Miss E. T. Brown). The lancet leaves are replaced by rather slender leafy stems and the oval lozenges, set off by changes in the color of their grounds, are filled in this instance with only one of the motives which we mentioned above, and these again are connected in their turn, one to another, through a second system of vines. After further evolution we find several diamond-trellises mutually inter-secting upon a uniform ground: blue, as a rule. These elements are formed of slender vines upon which the same motives, in what looks like an arbitrary arrangement, actually take their places according to a well-studied plan. Their relationship to the lively color contrasts which we have seen in the preceding phase is observed to the extent that the palmettes, rosettes, lilies etc., as they branch outwards from the central vertical axis, actually do correspond closely with their mates in drawing, but in every instance the colors differ completely. The marvelous ability of the Persian weaver of the classic period to improvise in the course of his work found eloquent expression in such glorious productions. Lady Baillie owns the most beautiful carpet of this kind; it had its exact counterpart in Berlin (Islamic Section), which we must sadly put down as another war loss (Fig. 97).

Then there is a more numerous series of vase rugs, undoubtedly later in date, and ordinarily with a red ground, which are laid out in the same manner as the last. In these, however, symmetry is not limited to the drawing, but is extended to the choice of colors as well. We discover an exception in the surviving fragment of what has been one of the most magnificent representatives of the vase-category, in the Vienna Museum. In this design the customary ornamental forms are borne upon stems which cross each other forming great pointed ovals, and the white field receives

97. So-called Vase Carpet (destroyed)   *Formerly State Museums, Berlin*

additional animation from minute blossom-work on delicate spiral vines
(Fig. 98). Here, just as in a fragment in the Victoria and Albert Museum,
we can pick out lancet leaves once more. In this case they do not to be sure
have an organizing function as previously, but are modeled very

unassumingly as vine sprouts; later on they gain in importance inasmuch as, when developed more richly and become boldly sweeping, they bring a whirling turbulence into the field which was once so serene. From this scene, moreover, the vases and the lilies have now been crowded out again (examples in the Corcoran Gallery and in the Gulbenkian Collection, etc., Survey Pl. 1234—1236).

On the other hand a type appears — in the 17th century for the first, in fact — in which the motif of the vase with flowers alone, arranged with several modifications in horizontal rows, dominates the entire surface. This occurs in a large carpet with a green ground in the Austrian Museum, whose undulating border is astonishingly loose in treatment when we contrast it with the dense ornamentation of the field (Fig. 99). Again, in other instances, the employment of multifoiled figures quite closely approaches the arrangement which we found in the compartment carpets; an example in this context is presented us by a carpet 24'6" in length in the Victoria and Albert Museum, in which one will note but a single diminutive vase, well hidden (Survey Pl. 1237). More important still, even though in ruinous condition, is a fragment in the museum at Sarajevo, which exhibits in diagonal rows oval panels filled with large palmettes or with cloud bands, upon a ground of more delicate blossom-work and tied together by a vine system which is indicated very faintly indeed. This piece has documentary value due to the presence of the signature of the master (Mu'min ibn Qutb ed-dîn Mâhâni) and the date A. H. 1067 (1656 A. D.; Survey Pl. 1238).

All of the vase carpets of the classical period have an elongated format and remarkably narrow borders. From this and from the progressive handling of their decorative scheme we must conclude that they were not intended to lie individually, but several of them side by side in a great hall, as for instance in the prayer area of a mosque, for which their limitation to floral forms would make them especially appropriate. Among their border designs one most frequently finds a rotation of small rosettes and palmettes with square clusters of tiny blossoms (Figs. 95—97). More rarely, arabesque trails occur which only upon the most rare occasions are stepped up into a broader and heavier treatment (Fig. 98).

As to their chronological sequence, the dating of the Sarajevo fragment, which undoubtedly stands at the very close of their development, provides the proof desired. To judge from this, the carpets with gay color contrasts

98. So-called Vase Carpet (fragment)
Austrian Museum of Applied Arts, Vienna

must have been produced by about the middle and those in which symmetry has been stressed, towards the end of the 16th century, with such examples as diverge from the original scheme to be credited to the first half of the 17th century. The question of where they were made remains still unsolved.

99. So-called Vase Carpet   *Austrian Museum of Applied Arts, Vienna*

Most writers are inclined to regard Kirman in Southeastern Iran as the birthplace of these vase carpets. This city is well attested as a place where rugs were produced, and it has been linked with the names of several master weavers, at least from the 18th century on. This thesis may appear

138

more plausible than the attribution to Joshaghan (northerly from Ispahan) which has been supplied by A. U. Pope. But this does not solve the problem of the undeniable relationship of the earlier diamond-trellis treatment to

100. "Shrub Carpet" (fragment)   *Musée des Arts Décoratifs, Paris*

that of the so-called dragon carpets; at the very least we must assume that some emigration of Caucasian weavers to Kirman had taken place.

Closely allied to the vase carpets is the category of the so-called *shrub* and *tree* carpets, which were certainly produced for the most part in the same center. A fragment in the Museum of Decorative Arts in Paris will be

139

found to be very informative in this respect. This piece has a continuous patterning of arabesque-ovals — in lieu of diamonds — in which, in addition to the shrubs and bushes, which are very diverse botanically, once more a vase is depicted in precisely the same concept as was customary in the class which we have just reviewed. With its gracefully undulant border of arabesques, this piece perhaps should still be placed in the 16th century (Fig. 100); a fragment in the Boston Museum may well have formed part of

101. "Tree Rug"   State Museums, Berlin

the same rug. Moreover, an additional specimen from the Sarre Collection is most closely akin to these. In the few surviving examples we can observe how in the course of the 17th century the handling of the shrubs grows gradually stiffer and how the motives ultimately become impoverished.

An interesting variety of progressive composition is offered us by a rather small rug in the Berlin Museum, in which leafy and flowering trees with pairs of birds upon them alternate with each other in transposed rows

140

without any compositional demarcation, within a very narrow border of rosettes and buds. This still dates from the first half of the 17th century and presumably is South Persian in origin (Fig. 101). About a century older and closely related to the Northwest Persian animal designs is the only known carpet of its type, that in the Williams Collection in Philadelphia, with

102. "Tree Rug"   *Formerly Dr. Jakob Goldschmidt, New York*

towering cypresses, various other kinds of trees and single palmette-flowers in its field, as well as roughly-drawn interpenetrating arabesque bands in its broad border (3rd edit., Fig. 40). A 17th century specimen of the late Dr. Jakob Goldschmidt's occupies a position intermediate between the two examples last mentioned; the singular cloud band border has visibly presented difficulties for the weaver, especially at the corners, where his attempts to find a solution have miscarried obviously (Fig. 102).

141

103. So-called Tree Rug in Silk (1671)
Mausoleum at Kum, Persia

In the Mausoleum of Shah Abbas II in Kum, the sarcophagus of the sovereign is covered by a row of identically drawn small tree rugs similar in pattern to those which we have just examined. One of these (Fig. 103) provides the name of the master weaver, Ni'matullah of Joshaghan, and the date A. H. 1082 (1671 A. D.). This designation of the origins of the fabricator has provided an argument for the association of whole categories of rugs with this place, although it offers no conclusive basis for such assumptions, since the master in question could naturally have done his work just as easily in Kirman or in Kashan. Kashan enters into the picture inasmuch as the entire Kum series is knotted in silk, whereas the design — in subdued tones upon a brilliant green ground, with a very narrow border indeed — might speak rather for Kirman.

Progressive design originally was standard also among the so-called *garden* rugs, which bear this name with justice; for in a very charming way they represent those architectonic garden layouts which are so characteristic of Persia, in textile formalization. We become conscious of great canals and of little ones that branch off from these, interrupted by basins or by planted platforms, accompanied by malls and enclosed by flower borders. Fishes or ducks swim in the water, and in earlier examples animals move about between the trees. An interesting large fragment of this class, which has now dropped completely out of sight, with exceptionally rich store of fauna and flora in a symmetrical arrangement, is

142

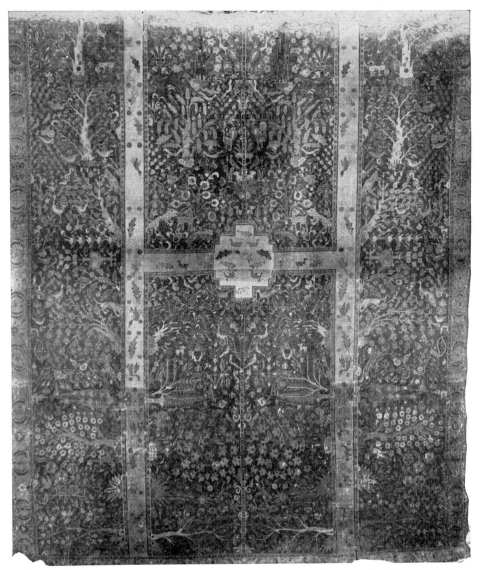

104. Garden Rug   *Formerly R. Wagner, Berlin*

related to those tree carpets of the 17th century which have been traced
back to Kirman (Fig. 104); we might give a somewhat earlier dating to the
well-known small example from the Figdor Collection (now in the Austrian
Museum), with a rather obscure orientation for its motives, some of which
are caught up in medallions.

Quite typical of the class are those garden rugs which are drawn more
stiffly, "architectonically", if we may say it, and of these Lord Aberconway

143

105. Garden Carpet   *Kevorkian Foundation, New York*

owns the most stately specimen (31'2″ × 11'8″, Survey Pl. 1270). Another, approximately as large, belongs to the Kevorkian Foundation. Its central watercourse is interrupted five separate times by islands with trees and side canals (Fig. 105). A large fragment of a third, a blend of red, green and blue, acquired by the Berlin Islamic Collection in 1920 from a Shiite shrine

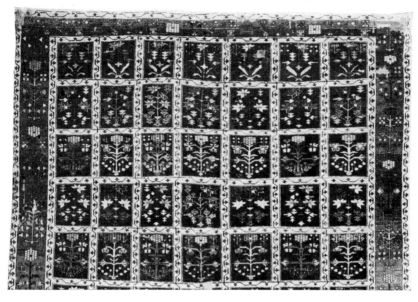

106. Garden Rug   *State Museums, Berlin*

in Iraq, unfortunately was destroyed in 1945. Specimens in a smaller format, which turn up rather often, seem like segments of such rugs. In these pieces the design sometimes appears centralized and is enclosed by the reciprocal crenellated border which we find so popular elsewhere too. The whole group is strictly homogeneous; it extends from the end of the 17th for some way into the early 18th century, and on account of the extremely severe treatment of its contours it has occasionally been taken for Caucasian or Armenian; more recently, Kurdistan has been suggested as the district where it originated.

A rug with a charming color scheme in the Berlin State Museum, very definitely mid-18th century, shows the connection between garden rugs and tree rugs: the field is divided up into 84 (7 × 12) square plots, which are separated by narrow footpaths, and each of these plots contains a severely stylized tree motive; one of these motives repeats in the border in such a manner as to emphasize the progressive orientation of the rug (Fig. 106).

Pictorial Rugs

Among rugs of progressive composition, animal designs evidently have always been very rare. A large fragment in Berlin, quite unique in its own fashion, but rather threadbare, cannot be admitted as a representative of that class without objection, for although the decorative scheme certainly does build up from one end of the rug to the other, still, despite its lateral repetition of motives in reverse, the symmetry of the design has not been maintained strictly. It is much more a matter of the two halves having been united by means of intermediate motives to create a uniform pictorial effect (Fig. 107). In addition to the representations of various animals assailing one another, already so familiar to us, we encounter several exceptional species of kylins, pairs of battling camels — in accordance with a favorite composition of the famous Bihzad — and bears (?) walking about erect, in a tangle of trees and shrubbery. The border has palmette and rosette blossoms upon arabesque bands and suggests a late 16th century dating. An incomplete animal carpet owned by Mr. John D. Rockefeller Jr. departs from the usual scheme in quite a different way: here upon a red ground over a background of flowering vines several kinds of animals are depicted in horizontal rows, repeated at intervals and all in motion towards the left. The composition is framed by a tripartite cartouche border (Survey Pl. 1182/83).

As a pictorial rug in the true sense, freed from all the laws of symmetry, yet with a well-balanced arrangement of its surface too, a specimen from the Altman Collection, knotted in silk, presents itself (Fig. 108). This piece reveals quite extraordinary ability both in its design and in its execution, and it certainly originated on the court looms of Kashan. Its border is of palmettes flanked by pheasants, as we have seen in other products of that center. A scenic rug of wool with hunters afoot and on horseback and with episodes from Persian romance (Laila and Majnun, Khusrau and Shirin) is in the Museum of Decorative Arts in Paris; the wide border displays, among animal combats, palmettes with genii and lobed medallions with seated figures.

The rugs listed here, each a great rarity of its kind, still belong collectively to the 16th century. It must be taken for granted that later on,

107. Animal Carpet with Progressive Design (fragment)   *State Museums, Berlin*

108. Pictorial Rug in Silk   *Metropolitan Museum, New York*

as well, the manufacture of this sort of "knotted paintings" formed a part of the standing repertoire in Kashan and in Kirman also; in the 19th century this led to a mass production of compositions which at times became utterly fantastic, and which were intended primarily for the European market.

The So-called Polonaise Rugs

Among the most luxurious products of the Persian court manufactories of the Safavid era we must include an additional class of rugs, which display their ornamental scheme in brilliant tints. Despite their costliness — for as a rule they are worked up in silk against a ground of silver or gold threads — they are still preserved in remarkable abundance. These are the so-called Polonaise rugs. This attribution stemmed from the Paris World Exposition of 1878, in which various specimens of this kind sent by Prince Czartoryski (they are now in the University Museum at Cracow) were exhibited, among which there were a few which bore the arms of his family. Actually, students believed that they could also make out in the border the letter M, which was explained as the hallmark of the Mazarski factory in Slucz. In this factory in the 18th century, demonstrably, were woven the Polish brocaded sashes, whose technique and design distinctly recall Persian silk-weavings, and for which the artisans were obtained from Iran at the start. However, the idea that any carpets were also produced either in Slucz or in Cracow was a delusion. The comparatively great number of examples extant (more than a hundred of them can still be instanced), the expensiveness of their materials and the extreme virtuosity of their technique permit us to infer a prosperity in the carpet industry, for which the necessary conditions were simply non-existent in Poland at that time. What is more, we can in fact follow this class back as far as the commencement of the 17th century at the very least, and consequently a full hundred years before Mazarski and his silk industry.

The true source of these rugs appears to be quite fully assured by the character of the decor, which is Persian throughout. Often this accords with the ornamentation of the medallion or of the arabesque carpets, yet at times it develops its own compositions too. The field, which frequently has a central star in the customary fashion, and now and then the corresponding corner devices as well, shows every floral motive subject to a characteristic stylization: the peculiar arabesque, so reminiscent of a brandished halberd, the full peony-palmettes, the tiny peach blossoms etc. on ornamental vines, amid which the cloud band in its various guises often weaves its way. Nevertheless, the design is less clearly marked than in the true medallion carpets and in the course of time it becomes somewhat confused.

109. "Polonaise" Rug   *Prince Liechtenstein, Vienna*

The effect aimed at in these rugs is a purely picturesque one, and when they are still in good condition it is that of baroque splendor. The rather loose knotting, the length of the pile, the interruption of the surface by broad areas of embroidered silver and gold thread, which create a background lying at a deeper level, together provide a rich pyrotechnic display of flashing lights in delicate but brilliant hues. The casual and even sleazy technique, as compared with other Persian silk rugs, of course makes these pieces less resistant to wear, so that only a relative few are found to be in perfect preservation. They hardly were to be considered seriously as floor coverings, and indeed they served as such only upon particular occasions. The border shows either a floral interchange, with arabesques or without them, or else the incised crenellated ornament which has been designated as the "reciprocal fleur-de-lis pattern", and which we have observed in other 16th—17th century rugs. The drawing and stylization of the flowers and of the other ornaments show that the greater part of the class were made in the 17th century. Individual pieces, especially certain ones whose borders have been designed forcefully albeit carefully, such as one rug that was formerly owned by Vincent Robinson and another belonging to Prince Johann Liechtenstein (Fig. 109), may well have been produced as early as around 1600. Others whose decor is quite disordered may not have come before the outset of the 18th century.

The relationships of these rugs to the rest of the Safavid carpets encourage us to conclude that they derived from one of the Persian court manufactories. The majority of the surviving pieces came to light in Poland, Austria-Hungary, Russia, in Turkey and in various princely households. In these they can often be followed back as far as the 18th and even on into the 17th century in the possession of the same family, whereas in Persia they are scarcely to be found at all. In any case they have not been brought to Europe from that country in the regular channels of trade. During the Vienna Carpet Exhibition, when dozens of "Polish" rugs, many of them of great beauty (the property of the Emperor of Austria, the King of Saxony, the Austrian Museum, and of Prince Liechtenstein, Baron Nathaniel and Baron Adolphe Rothschild, Prince Schwarzenberg, Count Schönborn etc.), were placed on show, the conclusion was reached that the place of their manufacture must be sought in Constantinople, or at least in the neighborhood of the Ottoman capital, where a well-developed silk industry was flourishing at the time.

This hypothesis too has long since been abandoned, and by the time of the Munich Exhibition of 1910, for which the first impetus was given through Prince Rupprecht by the discovery of a whole collection of such rugs in the Residenz, their Persian provenience could indeed be doubted no longer. The fact that they simply do not exist in their own native land can be accounted for in this way, that we are dealing here with a class of art objects which were made primarily to be sent to European courts as gifts from Shah Abbas I and his closest successors. The appearance of coats-of-

151

arms and an occasional concession to the Occidental taste of the day will then no longer seem astonishing, no more the fact that they proved at once to be equally desirable as articles of commerce. The court looms upon which they were manufactured presumably existed in the capital, Ispahan, itself or in its closest environs (hardly in Joshaghan, as A. U. Pope assumes).

110. "Polonaise" Rug   *St. Mark's, Venice. Alinari Photo*

In the Barberini Palace there were at one time a number of rugs of this description which had come there as presents for Pope Urban VIII; others (of like origin) were owned by the Colonna, Corsini and other Roman families. An exceptionally beautiful piece, superb in its color effect and in excellent condition, is owned by the Correr Museum in Venice; probably it belongs, together with sundry others in the Museum of San Marco, to that series which an ambassador from the Shah delivered to the Doge Grimani in 1603 (Fig. 110). Furthermore, in 1639 "Polish" rugs were brought to the

111. "Polonaise" Rug (destroyed)   *Formerly Kestner-Museum, Hannover*

Duke of Holstein-Gottorp by a Persian embassy; three of them were formerly at Glücksburg Castle. Others, including embroidered ones, are still to this day in Rosenborg Castle in Copenhagen and have been published by

112. "Polonaise" Rug   *Metropolitan Museum, New York*

F. R. Martin. In the Provincial Museum at Hanover there hung an especially handsome specimen, now destroyed, very freely and quaintly drawn, with green field and salmon-colored border, likewise quite obviously a gift to

154

the court established there (Fig. 111). Additional odd pieces have come to light in the Imperial Armory at Moscow, in Prussian court-ownership and in several Swedish castles. Today we can cite dozens of Polonaise rugs in American hands (some of them from the former Yerkes Collection); the most attractive of these surely are several in the Metropolitan Museum, a gift of John D. Rockefeller Jr. (Fig. 112; another specimen has a more distinct compartmentation). A pair of first-rate examples in excellent preservation are in the National Museum at Munich, still others in the

113. "Polonaise" Rug   *Formerly Figdor Collection, Vienna*

Victoria and Albert Museum. One, which dates from the late 17th century, decorated in a very unusual way with representations of animal combats among trees and treated in textile fashion as two identical lengthwise strips, will prove a surprise among those of the Royal Palace at Munich. A rug formerly in the Figdor Collection (Fig. 113) is sparsely ornamented with motives which are repeated in horizontal rows in a most peculiar manner, and is framed by a crenellated border; another and similar piece has been in Skokloster since 1653.

It is quite understandable that "Polish" rugs should be difficult to authenticate in paintings, since for such articles of luxury, when they appeared at all in trade, an artist's purse could scarcely have proved adequate. Even so, in a male portrait by G. Pencz in the Berlin Gallery (dated 1534) a rug that has been spread out over the table comes very

155

close to this class in its coloring. This would move their advent along up to well before 1550. Similar rugs may well have been depicted also in certain paintings by Terborch, Metsu, Dou and other Hollanders, and a woodcut by Jost Amman (about 1570), which shows several pieces with kindred ornamentation thrown over a parapet (Fig. 114), gives grounds for the same presumption.

114. Detail from a Woodcut by Jost Amman

Certainly carpets have also been knotted in Poland itself, as we know, and a few of these may well have appeared soon after 1700; however, they have a "folk-art" character which is fully Occidental, they are always of wool, are extremely crude both in their technique and in their drawing, and above all in their coloring too they bear no resemblance whatever to the patently refined products which we have just reviewed.

If we employ the term, "Polonaise rugs", which we have by now seen to be by no means pertinent, in the broader sense that thereby we are simply to understand works which were produced for Europe under the Safavids, then we must extend it so as to include as well those tapestry-woven, napless rugs which shared the same destination with the knotted ones, except that these naturally were planned as wall-hangings from the start. At the exhibition in Munich in 1910 this type was displayed in considerable numbers for the first time, and the Bavarian Court itself was able to contribute some of the most interesting examples. Among these was one which bore an escutcheon containing the Polish eagle and had come to the House of Wittelsbach by inheritance. In their decor these "kilims", which are carried out entirely in silk, occasionally experience the interpolation of silver threads and are distinguished by a rich and lively color scale. Often they take individual turns. Animal representations are particularly abundant in these pieces and even hunting scenes, genii and other imaginative motives are by no means rare. Since, however, we are dealing here exclusively with knotted rugs, these charming pieces do not fall within the scope of this handbook. Therefore we must content ourselves with calling especial attention to one of the Berlin Islamic Museum's specimens which has dragon and phoenix in its centerpiece, because of its documentary significance; for in four places we can pick out the word "pâdishâhi" (imperial), from which we may safely conclude that such pieces as these stemmed from a court manufactory. Today it is admitted generally, and quite rightfully, that this was the one that was active at Kashan.

Prayer Rugs

It may have been a comparatively early practice to use small rugs, which could be conveniently carried and stretched out upon the ground, for the performance of prayer when outside of the mosques, instead of the mats and embroidered or flat-woven fabrics which were customary otherwise. And it is no cause for astonishment that the thought should have occurred to someone of indicating in these products the niched form of the mihrab, which in the mosques themselves defined the kiblah, i. e. the direction towards Mecca. We do not know in what area the use of such prayer rugs began, but it could scarcely have been in Persia, where to this very day it has had no success that would approach the degree to which it has been favored in Anatolia.

The earliest example of a prayer rug that we can discover is in a Persian miniature dated 1436 in the Paris National Library (Fig. 115). The arch of the niche encompasses a field filled with squares or lozenges arranged in rows, the spandrels have blossom-work, and the narrow border, depicted only along the sides of the rug, is embellished with a simple trailing vine. A type similar to this must therefore have been already in use in the 15th century.

Of such original pieces as still survive, the earliest, which might be assigned to about 1500, show several niches placed side by side or else one above the other in a singular manner. Thus they belong to the category of the mis-named "family prayer rugs", which probably served primarily as floor pieces in the mosques. In these either the niche is enlivened only by a stepped medallion on a monochrome ground or else it is divided in two. In the latter case the head of the arch is kept quite plain, with

157

arabesques in the spandrels, in contrast to the lower half, which is adorned with dense blossoming vines. As a rule the borders have some cartouche arrangement. In a later variant of this kind, from the 17th century, both of the niches are entirely filled with floral decoration (Fig. 116).

115. Detail from a Miniature Painting (1436)
National Library, Paris

In the course of the 16th century it seems to have become usual for the spandrels as well as the upper portion of the border and guards to be embellished with quotations from the Koran and other pious texts. These were not carried all the way around the rug, for if they had been, the true believer would have necessarily turned his back upon some of them while in the act of praying. The niche itself, then, is filled with arabesques or cloud bands among blossoming vines, and the lower half of the border likewise has floral decoration of various kinds (Fig. 117). Still, the number of Persian prayer rugs that can be ascribed to the golden age of the 16th—17th centuries with any assurance is limited indeed, and their assignment to definite production centers creates even more difficulty than is the case with carpets of large dimensions. Several of them are embroidered with metal threads or are knotted wholly in silk and well-characterized thereby as articles of luxury.

The classical period is claimed, probably unjustly, for a whole series of prayer rugs in an excellent state of preservation, some 35 of which are still to be found in the Old Saray in Istanbul. Others, obviously from the same source, came into the trade long since and have made their way into public and private collections. Most of these adhere strictly to the type just described, worthy texts and all, but through the use of harder wool they have a different color harmony which is essentially non-Persian. Others make use of motives which have evidently been borrowed from Ottoman art, now and then even from Anatolian rugs of the 17th—18th centuries. However, as all of them, taken together, form a uniform category on a

116. Prayer Rug with Two Niches
Metropolitan Museum, New York

159

purely technical basis, the suggestion seems warranted that they have emerged collectively from some Turkish court manufactory of the 18th century, which copied or metamorphosed Persian designs with great dexterity.

117. Prayer Rug   *Formerly M. Indjoudjian, Paris*

MOGUL RUGS FROM INDIA

Turkoman rugs are much in demand today, and quite rightly so, in view of their perfection as handicrafts, their warm color tones and their sharp drawing. Their mother-countries perhaps are to be regarded as those of the art of rug-knotting generally. Still, we must dismiss these pieces completely from consideration in this book, inasmuch as we can scarcely trace them back as far as the 18th century. However, in the area of Samarkand and Bokhara, since the times of Tamerlane and his successors, the tribesmen may have developed the technique beyond that of a mere nomadic folk-art to a high state of refinement. From there it came, with Baber's dynasty which had been expelled from its seats of government in Western Turkestan and which henceforth was to found the empire of the Grand Moguls of Delhi, to India, along with the art of miniature painting, the manufacture of velvets and other arts as well.

Formerly, and it was still the case when the first edition of this hand-book appeared, to the Persian carpets of the classical era there was added a certain group of products which had obviously been developed at the very same time, i. e. in the 16th and 17th centuries. They show an assured stylistic consanguinity with the Safavid carpets, but form a distinct class of their own in view of certain peculiarities of design and coloring. Later on we were able to assign these pieces positively to a homeland in Northern India. In fact this class has been readily designated as "Indo-Persian", as this term serves to underline the fact that we here are essentially dealing with what amounts to an offshoot of Persian art upon Indian soil.

As our earliest example (still in the neighborhood of 1500) we make the acquaintance of a fantastic animal carpet, two fragments of which were reunited at the Munich Exhibition; since that time additional pieces have come to the surface, some of them probably from a second specimen. They all display upon a wine-red ground a singular decorative scheme of grotesque animal forms of every sort which spew one another forth in a mad swirl. The fragments are scattered among various museums (The Louvre, Washington, Detroit, St. Louis) and in private collections (Fig. 118). This motive, which traces back unmistakably to Indian symbolism, is afterwards revived in a delicate piece in the Musée des Arts Décoratifs,

118. Indian Animal Carpet (fragment)   *Formerly Loewenfeld, Paris*

with animal-heads on vines, and to this in turn conforms a smaller fragment in Boston.

The Mogul looms are shown in their full maturity in several carpets, some of which are purely floral, while others are enlivened with animals, but always drawn very naturalistically. Of these, the Museum in Vienna

162

possesses two of the most beautiful specimens. In the first (Sarre-Trenkwald I, Pl. 35) among trees with exuberant foliage and shrubbery all manner of birds are moving about: peacocks, cranes, chickens, turtledoves, hoopoes, partridges and the like, kept very true to nature and arranged with the greatest of freedom. Here the field has completely lost its textile character; more clearly still than in the Persian scenic rugs it is planned with an utter lack of symmetry, without any sort of tectonic restraint, and it is the border alone that still calls to mind the stricter style of the Safavid carpets: great palmette-blossoms with lion-masks on undulating stems which are interrupted by tiny snarling leopards and bellowing steers. In its buoyant, picturesque treatment the design reminds us of certain Persian and Indian lacquered book-bindings of the 16th/17th centuries, which evidently served as models. A similar *piece de luxe* with a wild hunt of all sorts of East Asian and Indian animals may be found in the Museum at Boston (Fig. 119). In addition to the wild beasts and a fantastic mythical creature, this composition offers us an ox-drawn cart containing a hunting leopard and a quick glance at life in a garden pavilion, all in a thoroughly untrammeled, picturesque portrayal. The border has palmettes with animal-masks. Akin to both of these, but with a decorative scheme which is somewhat more economical and hence less crowded, are a few animal carpets from the former Goupil and Yerkes Collections, others in the London and Paris museums of decorative art and in the Textile Museum in Washington, which also owns a fragment from the Sarre Collection, with two elephants standing face to face in beautiful draftsmanship. There is a carpet, formerly in the Widener Collection, which displays in its field, amid extravagant, highly agitated animal forms, an elephant striding serenely along with his rider, the whole enclosed by a classical border of cartouches and quatrefoils (Fig. 120).

The second of the Vienna Museum's choice pieces (Fig. 121) is characterized as a prayer rug by its niched construction. The appropriation of animate motives was of course forbidden on religious grounds, and so the field is simply filled up with many tightly-packed flowers, which all mount upwards, full and luxuriant and with delicate color harmonies, from a single bush. Another mihrab design, with a simple, loosely-drawn flowering shrub, is represented in several collections (among others, the Worcester Art Museum) and is found again in a more or less identical form in Persian brocades.

119. Mogul Scenic Rug   *Museum of Fine Arts, Boston*

120. Mogul Pictorial Carpet   *National Gallery, Washington*

121. Mogul Prayer Rug   *Austrian Museum of Applied Arts, Vienna*

122. Mogul Carpet   *Museum of Islamic Art, Istanbul*

For the identification of Mogul carpets, as a rule our standard clue is a
ground of a wine-red shade which is intrinsically dissimilar to those
nuances which are customary in Persia; just as typical an attribute of
Mogul carpets is the frequent very extensive disregard of symmetry, as we
have seen. However, this is not characteristic of those which have purely
floral decoration, in which well-balanced composition results in quite
original designs (Fig. 122). On the other hand, one meets with examples in
which Indian design repeats itself in a strictly textile manner, so that we

167

can generally infer in these a later origin and influences from the velvet industry which in the 17th century was well-developed in Northern India as well as in Persia. This dependence is certainly shown, for instance, in a silk rug in the Musée des Tissus at Lyons (3rd edit., Fig. 53) with flowering shrubs and birds, and even more distinctly in many other specimens whose fields we may find rather monotonous. In these last the entire decor is limited to unending rows of inconspicuous floral motives, to which even a border that is often somewhat stronger in its treatment is no longer able to impart much character as a carpet design. As regards mechanical execution, the employment of wool reaching sometimes the fineness of velvets, these very pieces as a class take their place among the most outstanding achievements of the art of knotting.

CONCLUDING REMARKS

The various classes of rugs which have been compiled in the foregoing chapters do not by any means exhaust the supply of old examples which has come down to us. In fact, among such original pieces as are known to us and among those copied in paintings, there are some that cannot be fitted accurately into any one of the groups put forward here; however, no specific reference has been made to these rugs in this book, inasmuch as they do not appear to be typical enough to warrant it. Then, too, there are certain of the older pieces which permit us to discern the deterioration of an established design or which are to be considered simply as incidental aberrations. Still others, from a certain hesitation in their drawing, must be regarded as timid transitional experiments at making the change-over from this scheme to that one. For if a strict observance of the esthetic requirements of style and technique is generally characteristic of carpet fabrication in the Orient right on down to the utter decadence of the whole line (i. e. until the middle of the 18th century), it has, even in the comparatively short period which we are in position to survey to some degree, shown repeated transformations, which were ushered in by certain symptoms of degeneration.

Up to now, as we have seen, we have but inadequate factual bases for a developmental history of the different patterns. The most important condition for this would be more precise information regarding the areas in which the various kinds of rugs were actually produced, and today this still is well-nigh entirely denied us. We can scarcely expect it to be amplified sufficiently for us in the future, either, as our literary sources are most obscure when they are not wholly lacking in data. Aside from these, next to nothing has been preserved as to region or spot. On the other hand, the modern rugs, among which localization is practicable in many cases — not invariably, despite the stunning assurance with which many a dealer is wont to classify each and every piece without hesitation — offer little serviceable evidence for us, as we have already noted. For with the decay

169

of the industry, which was not so much a failure of technique, but much rather a sort of esthetic collapse, such a barbarization and confusion of designs took place that any given piece, which we learn today to recognize as a product peculiar to one district or to another, rarely has resulted entirely from old traditions. To the contrary, it frequently has had no roots among the folkways of that people, but was taken up as something quite alien to local inheritance and then developed into a pure bazaar or home-trade item.

Now to be sure in his admirable carpet-history F. R. Martin already has made an attempt, drawing upon all sources at his disposal, to define more closely the localization of the old varieties of carpets, especially the Persian. Others have followed him in this experiment, but as enlightening as many of their hypotheses may have been, a general set of valid conclusions still are scarcely to be drawn from them, and in many an instance erroneous ideas now can certainly be pointed out. On this account we believe that for the present we must content ourselves merely with differentiating the great Near Eastern groups more sharply, one from another, and proceeding with a broader classification within these groups according to the ways in which their schemes of decoration have been laid out. A stylistic and regional relationship discloses itself automatically if we do this, wherever it is in the least evident (as for instance the connection between those medallion rugs which have animals and the ones that do not). Yet with our present stock of information it still appears too hazardous to set out to make a very definitive apportionment of the various Persian classes, for instance, among the known production centers. Kurt Erdmann has recently been endeavoring to obtain reasonably dependable and convincing evidence for such an allocation, as well as for their sequence chronologically, from the careful study of basic schemes of composition.

Accordingly, to begin with, we have only been able to present a quite general and limited view over the material at hand, the basis for which must be furnished by such dates as we actually do have and by certain critical hallmarks. In the previous editions, in order to accomplish this we started out with the products of the Persian Safavid era, which always have claimed particular interest. These have been very properly adjudged to be of obvious importance to any classification of carpets because of the character of their floral decor. In the design and the composition of these pieces a sound naturalistic perception vies with great stylistic power. The animal forms, as well as human figures exceptionally woven into the scheme, as a rule appear to be mere accessories, scattered over the flowery ground like figures in a landscape. Whereas at the outset design and draftsmanship still evince an almost stringent severity and, at times, even a certain meagerness in the forms, by about the middle of the 16th century these details have achieved a softer fullness, consummate taste in their distribution, buoyancy in their movement, fantasy in their conception and sumptuous color. Characteristic of this most sublime culmination of the Oriental art of knotting is, above all, the admixture of Chinese elements which, together with the other component parts of the decorative scheme, overflow into India as well, where this technique simultaneously attained to a similar climax. From the end of the 17th century with the break-up of the Safavid dynasty the designs start to become more simple; the drawing of the vegetation, amid which the animal figures again tend to disappear, becomes even more luxuriant, but at the same time more disordered and clumsy. On Turkish soil the classic Persian scheme of decoration undergoes final peculiar transformations in the 17th century, then becomes more and more misunderstood in the prayer rugs, and finally gushes forth in senseless distortion over the entire Near East.

In the 15th century the manufacture of carpets in Persia itself was preceded by an industry in the northwest frontier provinces of Armenia and the Caucasus which reveals distinctly its relationships with that of Iran. The designs show a wholly similar disposition: the floral decorative concept is standard here as well, but the drawing is stiffer and is inclined to freeze into geometric forms. If we follow this type of evolution back still farther, as from the 14th century on, let us say, an entirely different fashion attracts our notice, mostly in rugs as reproduced in paintings. The representation of animals steps into the foreground, and indeed forms the principal established motif of their decoration. Here they do not appear amid rich floral ornamentation for the mere enlivenment of the same, as in the carpets of the Safavids, but rise alone or in pairs as a proper leitmotiv, large in scale and isolated, from the strong and tranquil fields of the meanly enframed panels, repeating in regular alignment. In their angular, stylized drawing they have quite the effect of heraldic beasts, and evidently too there must have been some symbolic meaning that originally has served as the basis for their being treated in this manner. We must seek the home-land of such rugs, which are to be referred to the period from the end of the

13th up to the beginning of the 15th century, with reasonable assurance in Asia Minor or else in the Caucasus. Here animal design seems to have conformed to a geometrically linear style which we are justified in regarding as the oldest decorative principle of the entire knotting technique and which we can point out in conjunction with Cufic script as early as the 13th century. In Persia as well it persisted into the 15th century and then in Asia Minor it was intermingled with floral decoration, most effectively in the so-called Holbein rugs of the 15th to the 17th centuries, in which the forms of vegetation are scarcely still recognizable as such. Again, the blend has a different quality altogether in the kaleidoscopic patterning of the Mamluk rugs, and it is in the Ushak groups that it is really least apparent.

The old rug patterns have been copied in the Orient itself in later years, sometimes in entirety, at others only in detail, yet as a rule both kinds of these modern imitations are no more than superficial. Not only is the entire effect altered by the greater precision in weaving and the more beautiful and luxurious coloring of the antiques, but there is marked change as well in the form of a series of seemingly unessential details which either are completely lacking in the new, or else have been misinterpreted in the copying. So when one has grown somewhat accustomed to the repertoire of forms as found in the classic rugs, he will perceive with comparative ease all sorts of small errors and contradictions, and will be able to identify too those pieces which should be considered as downright forgeries. These last — just as in other branches of art — naturally never attempt to copy any known original exactly, but borrow from related prototypes such motives as would ordinarily vary from rug to rug. Yet, in their appropriation of these same motives, as a rule they commit offenses against the old stylistic laws. Of course the folio volumes which have come out during the past few decades, with their outstanding color-reproductions and their accurate technical analyses, have thereby made possible such amazingly precise imitations that it requires greater experience than ever to detect the fraud, especially when old woolen yarns have been reused.

Rug fanciers will generally find it sufficient if they can impress distinctly upon their minds the characteristic hallmarks of the classical era. The most readily identified are the Persian carpets of the golden age; for the peculiarly Mongolian elements which they exhibit to a greater or lesser degree are characteristic of these rugs alone, and are totally lacking in others, especially in later pieces. This is the case not only for Chinese

172

fabulous creatures: the phoenix, the kylin and the dragon, as well as such symbolical animals as the stag, crane etc.; above all is it true of that symbol of immortality, the "Tchi", which frequently also appears as a fungus or conglobate sort of figure in as pure a coinage as in the very works of art of China itself. Generally, however, we see it stylized as the "cloud band", in which guise it first occurred in the Iranian World. Just as the rugs, other contemporary products too, such as miniature paintings, faïences, bronzes and textiles are interspersed with the most varied modifications of this motif, which has been disseminated from Persia ever since the 14th century and became known to the West as well.

Of very different ancestry, on the other hand, and to be claimed neither as Far Eastern nor as typical of Persia is the frequently employed "three globe motive", which was erroneously interpreted in the earlier editions of this handbook as the "Tchintamani", an emblem of Buddhism. In actual fact, here we are dealing with a recollection of the legendary leopard-skin in which the most ancient Iranian and Turanian rulers were said to have arrayed themselves. This now achieves remarkable popularity in the Turkish domains, developed heraldically into dot-, globe- or crescent-form. Often we find it combined with other shapes which have been explained mistakenly as "lightning flashes" or "shreds of cloud", but which are actually to be regarded, nevertheless, as reminiscences of a similarly traditional tiger-hide (see above, p. 53, Figs. 31, 32). This motif of stripes and spots is believed to have served as the badge of the world-conqueror Tamerlane, and it appears several times on the sumptuous garments of the Ottoman sultans in the Saray Museum in Istanbul. In any case it is especially characteristic of Turkish art of the 15th—17th centuries and during that interval it plays an important role in all branches of industrial activity.

The remarkable care with which artists observed the animal life of Iran in the flesh becomes particularly evident in those animal designs of the 16th century which we have previously described. Animal combats and sudden feral attacks, which often have been dramatically portrayed, trace back to Old-Iranian dualistic beliefs and were carried over by the Persians into Islamic art, which then passed them on to the Occident too. When human figures found application, it was with reference to the portrayal of life at court, in which the hunt took an especially favored place. One certainly must assume that carpets with episodes of this sort were made up to order in the state manufactories. Lastly, we will be able to verify positively in Persian miniature paintings the angelic genii which appear repeatedly, in a thoroughly human concept; the fact that these, just as all other figurate motives, trace back to the sketches of the book-illuminators has already been amplified in its appointed place.

However, as we have said, floral decoration was truly dominant at all times, and in this in turn were paramount two principal forms, the full floral palmette and the arabesque vine. Both are frequently drafted in a strongly architectural manner; both are old characteristic factors in the Saracenic vocabulary of ornament. The palmette appears to have evolved from the water lily, that lotus blossom which has been at home on the Nile and the Tigris as well as along the rivers of Eastern Asia since the first beginnings of art and which has proved itself vital and productive in the Asiatic form-world for thousands of years. Alternately fully open or else closed bud-fashion, large or small, in frofile or as seen from above, it constitutes the real basic element of design during the golden age of Persian art. Beside these are scattered flowers of various kinds (usually opened out to rosette shape) which are utilized to fill up the surface. Riegl in his "Stilfragen" has illustrated exhaustively the derivation of the arabesque, a new invention of Islamic art, from the late-antique leafy vine. Regardless of all technical difficulties, to artists at carpet-weaving it presented a magnificent opportunity to display their drafting skill in most tasteful delineations. In the border it tends to form a frame for the open flower, and in a similar arrangement the two frequently fill the field as well.

The botanical identification of the flowers or shrubs which appear beside the palmettes and rosettes in the older rugs is extremely difficult or quite impossible due to their stylization. The smaller blossoms resemble those of the apple tree, the peach or the almond; the larger, the lily. The more naturalistically handled flowers, especially tulips, carnations and hyacinths, which are most strikingly common in Ottoman rugs of the 17th century, bear the most marked relationship to the ornamentation of Isnik faïences and many brocades and velvets of the same period; these flowers seem to have been the general stock-in-trade of the various Turkish handicrafts of that time. Finally, the intensified geometrization of all plant forms, often to a point beyond all recognition, is characteristic of most classes of Anatolian rugs, yet of this phase in Persia we really possess but one example — and still regarding this one we cannot be absolutely

174

certain — in the crenellated variety of "reciprocal fleur-de-lis design", which has found particular employment as a border device among the so-called Polonaise rugs.

Of all the varied elements which leaven the rugs of the 16th and 17th centuries so profusely and so systematically, we find in the newer products, in so far as they still possess any original qualities at all: of Chinese motives, no further trace; of the pure Persian and of Saracenic in general, where these do occur, but a residue and misinterpreted at that. For this reason it is not difficult to differentiate the carpets with animal and floral ornamentation of the golden age, even from those copies of the first half of the 18th century which display these elements in the earliest stages of their barbarization, yet still in a certain pleasing relationship. With the progress of decadence the differences naturally also become more distinct. The case is altered when we come to those old varieties of rugs whose designs are composed of ribbon-interlaces and other geometric figures. This form of decoration is the best adapted for the knotting technique; therefore it occurs during all periods and its simple motives offer no footholds for the critic. It boils down to this, that these designs have been imitated with more or less fidelity in modern times, not only in places where old models have been expressly specified by European purchasing-agents, but often also where old traditional methods are actually involved which have been preserved free from adulteration. In such modern rugs we consequently find very expressive tokens of the older periods: plaited and coiled patterns, latch-hooked ornaments, six- or eight-sided panels with bar-like motives, reciprocal designs in the border, letter-forms and many another. Then too it is not rare for these devices to conform precisely, the new to the old, despite their considerable separation in time. The arrangement of the individual motives, the ratio of field to border and other stylistic criteria avail us but little, since in these respects a certain leeway was established in early times as well as in recent practice. The borders might often be kept very narrow indeed, but then again they might be made remarkably wide, or even doubled or tripled. In such cases one will most easily avoid mistakes by sticking to the colors, which are so purely and harmoniously blended in the products of the golden age that anyone who once has fully grasped the coloristic beauty of primitive rugs will straight-way be struck by their contrast with all later pieces — not to mention those which have been dyed with anilines.

THE PRINCIPAL BOOKS ON RUGS

The following selection will be found to include publications of general interest only to the extent that they deal with the aspect of the subject which is our present concern, and still are not as yet to be regarded as obsolete. Treatises and monographs on individual carpets have not been mentioned. Catalogs of museums and of individual collections have been taken up more or less as a class, but auction catalogs on the other hand have not. On principle we have taken no notice of those rug books which year by year have made their appearance in ever greater numbers as adjuncts of the trade, and which deal for the most part if not exclusively with modern carpets for everyday use, helpful as acquaintance with such volumes may prove also for anyone who is making an exhaustive study of the classical period of the art of knotting.

The sequence is arranged in such a way that those publications which cover the field inclusively are given first in their chronological order, and then the books which merely deal with portions of our subject.

F. R. MARTIN, A history of Oriental carpets before 1800. 2 vols., London, 1908.
> A basic work, and thus indispensable, with much of its material published for the first time in the form of excellent reproductions, many of them in color.
> Significant dates for the history of carpets are given, but among these many are in error, so they are to be used with caution only.

W. R. VALENTINER, Early Oriental rugs. New York, 1910.
> Published on the occasion of an exhibition in the Metropolitan Museum. This showing included 50 items, mostly American in ownership.

F. SARRE and F. R. MARTIN, Meisterwerke Muhammedanischer Kunst. Munich, 1912.
> Three large folio volumes which were put out in connection with the Munich Exhibition of 1910. The carpets are described and pictured in Vol. I, Pl. 42—88.

A. F. KENDRICK, Guide to the Collection of Carpets. Victoria & Albert Museum. London, 1920.
> Running text without detailed individual descriptions, containing 48 small plates.

A. F. KENDRICK and C. E. C. TATTERSALL, Hand-woven carpets, Oriental and European. London, 1922. 2 vols.
> In addition to carpets of the golden age, this work contains many late examples too, but little that is new in the way of research developments.

J. BRECK and F. MORRIS, The James F. Ballard Collection of Oriental Rugs. New York, 1923.
> 129 illustrations together with descriptions of those rugs of the Ballard Collection which were presented to the Metropolitan Museum. Among these there are also included prayer rugs dating from more recent times.

A. MAC LEAN, Catalogue of Oriental rugs in the Collection of James F. Ballard. St. Louis, 1924.
> Detailed listing with reproductions of 106 rugs which were not included among those which were bestowed upon the Metropolitan Museum. Most are Anatolian, 16th—18th centuries.

A. U. Pope, Catalogue of a loan exhibition of early Oriental carpets. The Art Club. Chicago, 1926.
Contains descriptions, illustrations and scholarly commentary as regards 54 important carpets of the classic period, of varied ownership.

F. Sarre and H. Trenkwald, Altorientalische Teppiche. Leipzig and Vienna, 1926—1928. 2 vols.
A great masterpiece with 60 outstanding plates, to a great extent in color, in each volume together with a penetrating analysis of each individual carpet. Introductory comments by Sarre, Trenkwald and Troll; bibliography by Erdmann. Vol. I includes the Vienna rugs only; Vol. II, carpets from various other collections. This publication has practically superseded the older Vienna folios (1892—95, 3 vols.).

H. Jacoby, Eine Sammlung orientalischer Teppiche. Berlin, 1927.
This collection, broken up long since, included, aside from many very usable carpets, a number of classic pieces of the 16th—17th centuries as well.

A. U. Dilley, Oriental Rugs and Carpets, a comprehensive study. New York, 1931.
With 79 plates, half of them antique rugs, 14 in color. A treasury of extremely useful information presented in very agreeable form by an experienced connoisseur.

M. S. Dimand, The Ballard Collection of Oriental Rugs in the City Art Museum of St. Louis. St. Louis, 1935.
This comprises the group of rugs, which had been published previously in part, that were given by this collector to the museum in St. Louis. Most are Anatolian.

K. Erdmann, Orientteppiche. Illustrated booklets of the Islamic Department, Berlin State Museum, No. 3. Berlin, 1935.
Short descriptions with 46 illustrations, some of them in color.

M. Campana, Il tappeto orientale. Milan, no date (1945).
Contains several unfamiliar examples of the older rugs owned in Italy and illustrations of rugs in paintings.

The Art Institute of Chicago, An Exhibition of Antique Oriental Rugs, 1947.
This included 114 carpets of varied provenance. 50 illustrations.

M. e V. Viale, Arazzi e tappeti antichi. Turin, 1948.
On the occasion of an exhibition in the Palazzo Madama in Turin. The first part comprises tapestry-weavings only; the second, Oriental rugs in about 50 plates, with a very conscientious text.

P. Otten, Tentoonstelling Oostersche Tapijten. Catalogus. Delft, 1949.
Small but interesting exhibition of 135 rugs, ancient and some of them previously unknown, lent by Dutch owners, with an introduction and 48 illustrations.

K. Erdmann, Orientalische Teppiche aus vier Jahrhunderten. Museum für Kunst und Gewerbe. Hamburg, 1950.
The important and scholarly catalog of an exhibition of carpets of German ownership, mostly of the classical period, including 155 numbers with 49 illustrations.

S. Troll, Altorientalische Teppiche. Österr. Museum für angewandte Kunst. Vienna, 1951.
Contains 46 small plates which present the most important items in the celebrated Viennese Collection and a general introduction.

K. Erdmann, Der orientalische Knüpfteppich. Versuch einer Darstellung seiner Geschichte. Tübingen, 1955.
Important as a short, but interesting discussion of the individual groups of rugs and of some general problems, presenting the author's own ideas, followed by a very copious bibliography. 179 illustrations in collotype and 8 color plates.

K. Erdmann, Der türkische Teppich des 15. Jahrhunderts. Istanbul, n. d. (1957).
> 81 pages with 67 illustrations. German text, followed by a Turkish translation, mainly intended for the author's Turkish students, dealing also with some earlier and later groups.

J. Vegh et Ch. Layer, Tapis turcs provenant des églises et collections de Transsylvanie. Paris, no date (1925).
> Illustrates Anatolian rugs of the 17th—18th centuries through the medium of 30 colored plates, without descriptions.

E. Schmutzler, Altorientalische Teppiche in Siebenbürgen. Leipzig, 1933.
> This volume deals with the Anatolian rugs which survive in churches or in private hands. 55 colored plates, with important points brought out in the text.

K. Erdmann, Orientalische Tierteppiche auf Bildern des XIV. und XV. Jahrhunderts. Jahrbuch der preuß. Kunstsammlungen, Vol. 50, 1929, pp. 261—98.
> An important compilation of the old animal carpets, with 44 illustrations. A supplement to this appeared in the same periodical for 1941, pp. 121—126.

C. J. Lamm, The Marby rug and some fragments of carpets found in Egypt. Orientsällskapets årsbok, 1937, pp. 52—130.
> Which treats of the early fragments exhumed at Fostât.

R. M. Riefstahl, Primitive Rugs of the "Konya" Type in the Mosque of Beyshehir. The Art Bulletin, Vol. XIII, No. 2, 1931, pp. 1—44.
> An important paper dealing with some rugs of the Konia and Ushak groups, with comparative material.

S. Troll, Damaskus-Teppiche. Ars Islamica IV, 1937, pp. 201—231.
> Deals with the problem presented by the Egyptian carpets, whose homogeneity he recognizes, but whose origin in Egypt itself he disputes. Table of technical analyses.

K. Erdmann, Kairener Teppiche I. Europäische und islamische Quellen des 15.—18. Jahrhunderts. Ars Islamic V, 1938, pp. 179—206. II. Mamluken- und Osmanenteppiche, op. cit. VII, 1940, pp. 55—82, with 22 illustrations.
> A basic treatise on the ascription of the so-called Damascus carpets to Egypt, with a recapitulation of all important evidence.

E. Kühnel and L. Bellinger, Catalogue of Cairene Rugs. The Textile Museum, Washington, 1957.
> Detailed descriptions of the 33 Egyptian carpets belonging to the Textile Museum together with introductory texts for the four groups. Technical analyses by L. Bellinger. 49 plates, of which 10 are in color.

The Textile Museum, Dragon Rugs. A loan exhibition from American public and private collections. Washington, 1948.
> A short listing of 37 Caucasian dragon rugs, of which some 30 are products of the 17th century, without descriptions. One illustration.

J. K. Mumford, The Yerkes Collection of Oriental rugs. New York, 1911.
> An important publication on the carpets, for the most part Persian and Indian, of this celebrated collection, long since dispersed. Individual descriptions of the 27 pieces, which have all been reproduced in color, but with unequal success.

M. S. Dimand, Persian rugs of the so-called Polish type. Metropolitan Museum, New York, 1930.
> On the occasion of a special showing, which included 27 numbers, with 8 plates.

178

A. U. Pope, Survey of Persian Art, The Art of carpet-making: History. London, 1938/39.
    Vol. III, pp. 2257—2465, Pl. 1107—1275, many of these in color.
    Fundamental among modern publications on the Persian carpets of the classical
    period, with a wealth of illustrative material. Includes a thorough discussion of all
    pertinent problems, with attempts at localizing types with greater precision. Briefer
    contributions by T. Mankowski and H. Jacoby. As an important critique and
    supplement to this, see the detailed review by K. Erdmann in Ars Islamica VIII,
    1941, pp. 121—191, with 23 illustrations.

A. Brigg, Timurid carpets. Ars Islamica VII, 1940, pp. 20—54 and XII/XIII, 1946, pp. 146—158.
    These studies treat of the geometric and medallion carpets of the 15th century as
    reproduced in Persian miniature paintings, with many illustrations.

TRANSLATOR'S NOTES

Note 1 (P. 29): Recent inheritors of the traditions of the Anatolian animal carpets may well include the so-called Verné bird and animal kilims of the Caucasus. Comparison of such a Verné as that illustrated as fig. 107 by Neugebauer and Orendi with a series of animal carpets in Italian paintings will bring out various similarities in the creatures portrayed. Pairs of eagles such as appear in fig. 6 of this book and fig. 8 of Erdmann's "Der orientalische Knüpfteppich" have evidently suffered transformation into a single beast with two heads and two long necks, between which still thrives the 14th century's shrub.

Note 2 (P. 37): Rugs of this third group of "Holbein" weavings are often distinguished as "Lotto" rugs, due to their incidence in certain of Lorenzo Lotto's paintings.

Note 3 (P. 53): The translator would like to enter his protest against a recent addition to rug mythology. In an otherwise estimable and widely circulated book, Transylvanian rugs have been termed "seven mountains" rugs. This appealing bit of mistranslation has since appeared in auction catalogs and has otherwise been reflected in the trade. "Siebenbürgen" can be translated as seven castles, seven fortresses, or even seven burghs or towns — but never as seven mountains.

Note 4 (P. 68): The McMullan compartment and tree rug mentioned is now in the Metropolitan Museum. In Mr. McMullan's own opinion, this class of carpets was produced in North Persia, possibly in the Herez district. He has also pointed out the resemblance of its motif in which four trees grow outwards from a single lobed octagon to that of the octagonal wooded islands or planted platforms in certain of the garden rugs (such as Erdmann, "Der orientalische Knüpfteppich", Fig. 123). Erdmann himself reminds us (in the same volume) that a buffer zone evidently existed between Tabriz and the Caucasus proper, and he feels that Caucasian influence gradually increased its force in this area in the course of the 17th century. To this district, under the nebulous and rather unsatisfactory term,

"Northwest Persian-Caucasian", he refers: this group of compartment and tree rugs; the abovementioned class of stylized garden rugs, often quite large; several stylized animal rugs (Arthur M. Brilant of New York City has a good example); the compartment rug shown as Fig. 92 of this book; sundry tree rugs and shrub rugs, and certain other types. Hybrid products from this part of the country which show the same complex of Persian forms and color subject to Caucasian geometry in varying degree still often appeared in the trade a generation ago, bearing such names as "Karaje" (Karadagh), "Serapi" (Sirab) and Karabagh.

Note 5 (P. 75): Fantastic as it may seem to our readers in view of historical considerations as well as past opinions on the matter, recognition of certain Far Eastern features in the Mamluk rugs has recently led the translator to explore the possibility that the Cairo manufactory had been initiated with master weavers drawn from the present Sinkiang area (Chinese Turkestan), or perhaps more directly from Samarkand, accross the Pamirs, if we can accept that a manufactory was active there for the embellishment of the Timurid court resident in that place. All of the details involved are somewhat distorted, as they would be at the hands of alien copyists. The thesis is perhaps unprovable, due to the total disappearance of entire classes of ancient rugs in both areas and inasmuch as it presupposes the existence of an important manufacture of long standing in Chinese Turkestan, probably at Khotan, regarding which we have no surviving record.

Sinkiang origin of the master weavers of Cairo would explain the presence in the Mamluk fabrics of the Senna form of knot and the satellite variety of centralized compositions, which were not practised over a considerable intervening area, to our best knowledge. Certain correspondences exist also between several of the older classes of Turkish rugs and those rather recent weavings from Eastern Turkestan and China proper which are available for our study. Here, however, it would appear more unlikely that weavers from the East had ever been employed in any capacity.

The translator hopes to publish his findings on these topics when he has had access to additional material and can develop his theme more fully than at present.

Note 6 (P. 84): It now seems likely that the author has been over-suspicious of the Siberian rug cited. This was found in Mound 5 of a group of kurgans in the Pazirik Valley in the river system of the Upper Ob.

Apparently the chieftain or "king" was of a people allied to the Scythians and sharing many elements of their art. This rug is now on display in the Hermitage Museum at Leningrad. To Erdmann the layout resembles that of a cover rather than a carpet for the floor. Dr. Rudenko has assigned it to a Persian workshop and has pointed out many details which he considers to be Assyrian in concept. In her recent book, "The Scythians", Tamara Talbot Rice suggests that certain features of the decoration, such as the presence of bands of animal ornament in one of which the creatures move in an opposite direction from that of the second, seem characteristic of Scythian art practices. In view of this, she feels that "it may have been made to the express order of a Pazirik chieftain". Unfortunately, Mrs. Rice repeats an error made in several previous publications in giving the knot count the quite incredible fineness of 2700 to the square inch. We are informed that the actual ratio is more nearly 225 to the square inch, which indeed is unusually fine weaving for the Ghiordes technique, regardless of period. From these several factors we might infer an extended history of rug knotting prior to the 5th century B. C. dating which has been offered for this piece. Granting always that the knotting is "Turkish", Erdmann states, "Further development thereafter must have been in reverse".

As we go to press, comparative evidence coming to light in Europe hints strongly that the dating for this Pazirik hoard has been greatly overstated and even that we may be dealing with objects which have been buried since the time of Christ.

Note 7 (P. 139): The assumption offered here, that an emigration of Caucasian weavers to Kirman might have influenced the resemblance between vase and dragon rug designs, fairly begs for additional discussion. We may well feel that the author has selected the right track, but that our style caravan had taken the opposite course along it. Perhaps the oldest surviving dragon rug does by some chain of accidents somewhat antedate the earliest vase carpet known to us. Still, design influence is prone to flow from a polished art to one which lacks for motives and sophistication. Earlier in the text (page 49) it has been suggested that the Caucasian pieces represent the translation of a theme into terms suitable for carpets to be woven with a coarser technique. Where would we look for finer knotting? Persia first comes to mind.

Yet before we over-hastily assign this theme to Kirman we must, as always, weigh the possibility that some group of earlier carpets no longer extant has sired not only the dragon and vase rug patterns but also others, perhaps indirectly (such as the lovely lost "Brussa" Ottoman Cairene, Fig. 52), one of a succession of bygone designs, at times reflected in the miniatures, from which the many heterogeneous old and recent lattice layouts which have appeared from Spain to China have gradually evolved.

Note 8 (General): A remarkable recent book, "Gothic Cathedrals and Sacred Geometry", by George Lesser of London, deals brilliantly with the applications to religious architecture from the Classical Era through the Middle Ages of the two geometrical layout methods, "constructio ad triangulum" and "constructio ad quadratum", which together constitute what has been known as "true measure". Upon reading this book, the translator was induced to use this approach upon a photograph of a noted Oriental rug — the Ballard Ottoman Cairene prayer rug in the Metropolitan Museum. The results were so rewarding that he has embarked upon a careful study, likewise very fruitful to date, of the various classes of antique rugs from this standpoint with an eye to eventual publication. These layout methods, used to provide a framework of lines and measures from which the designer might make his selections in confidence that his results would be esthetically satisfactory, apparently have never been the subject of formal notice as regards their effects upon carpet design.

Preliminary observation would seem to indicate that such methods have been employed throughout the normal range of knotted carpets, including those of China, and that careful draftsmanship in these terms has been as effective in establishing the early Konia patterns as for certain comparatively modern Turkish, Persian and Chinese rug designs.

The primary layout upon the basic measure of the field's width is, naturally, the easiest to determine, often a direct application with the length of the field or the length of the rug a function of this measure and the border widths a reflection of measurements taken from the telescoped or "core" polygons or "polygrams" which each system provides. A ready explanation for the difficulties experienced by Western merchants in obtaining new carpets woven in the exact dimensions thought most desirable in Occidental trade!

Centralized and scenic composition can be "proved out" in detail by the use of one or the other of these systems, and efforts will be made to determine the rules of thumb which have governed their application in the actual designing, as well as those which have been employed in working out repetitive patterns (evidently often composed with reference to a series of points or lines established in the borders).

It is hoped that this approach to the carpets will increase our understanding of the old pieces, through introducing a new basis for their study. We may find help with various problems still unresolved, as in making allocations or ascriptions to an individual master weaver and his pupils; we may be able to carry a given layout technique from one area to another; we may find it easier to conclude that certain manufactories or manufactures have been set up with designers who have paid little more than "lip service" to patterns previously characteristic of those areas. These and many other possibilities will be kept in mind, as well as similar manifestations in other branches of art in variours places, to the extent that material and time permit.